Army Badges and Insignia
Since 1945
Book One

U.S.A., Great Britain, Poland, Belgium,
Italy, U.S.S.R., German Federal and
Democratic Republics

To
my wife

Army Badges and Insignia
Since 1945
Book One

Great Britain, Poland, U.S.A., Italy,
German Federal and Democratic
Republics, U.S.S.R., Belgium

by

Guido Rosignoli

BLANDFORD PRESS
POOLE   DORSET

First published in 1973

© 1973, 1976 Blandford Press Ltd,
Link House, West St, Poole, Dorset BH15 1LL

ISBN 0 7137 0648 1

Reprinted 1976

Colour section printed in 4-colour lithography
by Colour Reproductions Ltd, Billericay
Text computer typeset in 10/10 Lumitype Plantin
Printed in Great Britain by Butler & Tanner Ltd,
Frome and London

Contents

Introduction

The research necessary for the publication of my first book, *Army Badges and Insignia of World War 2*, left me with a great deal of additional information regarding the badges of the same armies used after 1945. I soon discovered that thousands of entirely new badges had been adopted in these last twenty-eight years and so became fascinated by this new field.

Although the publishers have agreed to add a few more pages of illustrations to the present book, I regret that space limitations, once again, have compelled me to deal solely with the regular armies, although some territorial badges have been included in particular cases when, by so doing, I could simplify the subject.

The reader will certainly realise that if I had attempted to illustrate all the British badges, including those of the territorials, little room would have been left for other armies, thus marring the original concept of this publication. I hope that in future I will be able to compile a separate book dealing only with the badges of territorial units, in the case of Britain worn since 1908, which will enable me to illustrate and describe all the changes and reorganisations that have taken place since then.

The translation of the N.C.O.s' ranks again presented an extremely difficult task, particularly with regard to the German ranks, and, as Germany is divided with two separate Armies, I had no choice but to refer to their original German-language titles.

I would like to thank the many readers who have written to me, and to the publishers, for showing their appreciation of my previous book.

G. Rosignoli,
Farnham, Surrey, 1973

Acknowledgments

I would like to thank:

The Belgian Embassy and Major Davreux for their help with the Belgian chapter.

The Embassy of the Federal Republic of Germany.

Mr K. Barbarski for his untiring help and his translations.

Sergeant-Major David W. Bruce, for giving his invaluable assistance in the wide field of the American shoulder sleeve insignia.

Mr A. Mollo who gave me access to all his files and constantly advised me.

Geom. L. Granata, who helped me with the Italian chapter.

I especially appreciate the kind help of Mr F. Ollenschläger who has given me the benefit of his knowledge through all the chapters of this book.

I also appreciate the help given to me by Mr B. W. T. Cockcroft, Mr A. L. Kipling, Mr H. L. King, Captain J. C. Cochrane, the Royal Irish Rangers, Mr J. E. Hankin, Major Frank Croxford, Major H. P. Patterson, Curator of the Royal Green Jackets Museum and Lt.-Col. H. N. Cole, O.B.E., T.D.

Lastly, my most sincere thanks to my wife who patiently transformed my manuscript into the text of this book.

OFFICERS' RANK BADGES

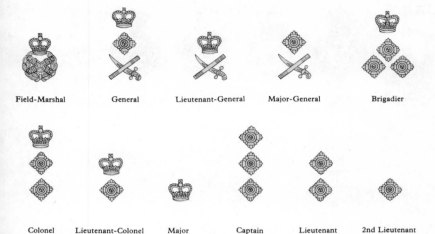

Field-Marshal | General | Lieutenant-General | Major-General | Brigadier

Colonel | Lieutenant-Colonel | Major | Captain | Lieutenant | 2nd Lieutenant

WARRANT OFFICERS' AND N.C.O.s' RANK BADGES

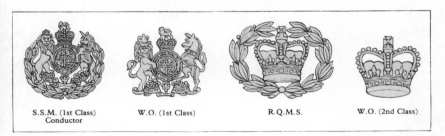

S.S.M. (1st Class) Conductor | W.O. (1st Class) | R.Q.M.S. | W.O. (2nd Class)

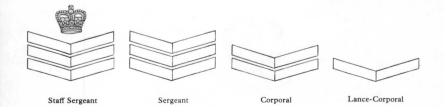

Staff Sergeant | Sergeant | Corporal | Lance-Corporal

PLATE 1

CAP BADGES
Household Cavalry and Armoured Cavalry Regiments

Royals

H.C.

L.G.

R.H.G.

B. & R.

Q.D.G.

R.S.D.G.

4/7 D.G.

5 Innis D.G.

Q.O.H.

Q.R.I.H.

9/12 L.

R.H.

13/18 H.

14/20 H.

15/19 H.

16/5 L.

17/21 L.

PLATE 2

CAP BADGES
Arms and Services

R.A.

R.T.R.

R.A.C.

R.E.

R. Sigs.

R.H.A.

R.A.O.C.

R.M.P.

R.A.M.C.

R.C.T.

M.P.S.C.

R.A.V.C.

R.E.M.E.

G.P.R.

A.A.C.

R.A.D.C.

R.A.E.C.

PLATE 3

CAP BADGES
Arms and Services

R.A.P.C.

R.P.C.

I.C.

A.P.T.C.

G.S.C.

P.R.

Junior Leaders
Trng Regt

A.C.C.

S.A.S.

M.D.C

Army Dept
Fire Service

Army Legal
Services

W.R.A.C.

Q.A.R.A.N.C.

Royal Hospital
Chelsea

PLATE 4

CAP BADGES
Miscellanea

Control Commission
Germany

Army Dept
Constabulary

Army Dept Police
Cyprus

R.M.A.
Sandhurst

Mons Officer
Cadet School

R.M.S.M.

Small Arms
School Corps

Foot Guards

Grenadiers

Coldstream

Scots

Irish

Welsh

PLATE 5

CAP BADGES
The Brigade of Gurkhas

2nd

6th

7th

10th

Transp. Regt

Engineers

Signals

Staff Band

G.M.P.

Infantry Regiments

R. Lincolns

R. Leicesters

R. Hamps.

Dorset

Green Howards

Wilts

R.B.

Manch.

K.O.Y.L.I.

PLATE 6

CAP BADGES
Brigades

Lowland

Home Counties

Lancastrian

Fusilier

Forester

East Anglian

Wessex

Light Infantry

Yorkshire

Mercian

Welsh

North Irish

Highland

Green Jackets

PLATE 7

CAP BADGES
Infantry Regiments

Queen's

R. Anglian

Yorkshire

K.O.R.B.

Worc. & Sherwood Foresters

Devon & Dorset

R.I.R.

Green Howards

Staffs

Duke of Ed.'s

R.H.F.

King's

Queen's Lancs

Glosters & Hamps.

Q.O. Hldrs

R.G.J.

PLATE 8

CAP BADGES

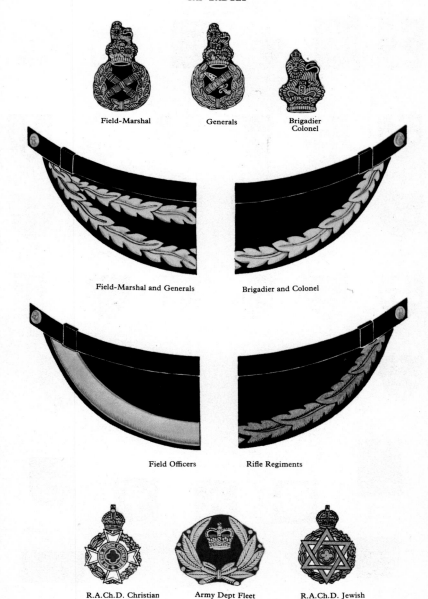

Field-Marshal

Generals

Brigadier
Colonel

Field-Marshal and Generals

Brigadier and Colonel

Field Officers

Rifle Regiments

R.A.Ch.D. Christian

Army Dept Fleet

R.A.Ch.D. Jewish

PLATE 9

FORMATION SIGNS

Home Commands

Scottish

H.Q.   Troops

Northern

Western

Eastern

South-Eastern

H.Q. Southern

Infantry

R.A.C.

R.A.

R.E.

R.A.O.C.

R.A.S.C.

R. Sigs

R.M.P.

R.A.M.C.

R.E.M.E.

R.A.P.C.

R.P.C.

I.C.

R.A.D.C.

A.C.C.

A.P.T.C.

R.A.E.C.

W.R.A.C.

Miscellaneous

R.A.D.C.

Northern and Eastern (1947)

Orkney and
Shetland Defences

Garrisons and other formations

East and West
Ridings Area

Edinburgh Garr.

Catterick Garr.

Force 135
Channel Islands-
Lib. Force

A.A. Command

Shoeburyness Garr.

Br. Troops in Northern Ireland

PLATE 10

FORMATION SIGNS

Districts

Northern Ireland (2)

North Wales

South Wales

West Scotland

Lancs and Border

West Lancashire

Salisbury Plain

London

North Highland

South Highland

North Riding

North Midland

South Midland

East Scotland

West Riding

Central Midland

East Anglian

Northumbrian

East Riding and Lincs

Norfolk and Cambridge

North Kent and Surrey (2)

Hants and Dorset

Sussex

East Kent

Northern Ireland

Northumbrian

East Anglian

South-Western

Aldershot

South-Western

PLATE 11

GREAT BRITAIN

FORMATION SIGNS
Army Corps

1st Corps

R.A.

R.E.

R. Sigs

R.A.S.C.

2nd Corps

Divisions

1st Division

R.A.

R. Sigs

R.A.S.C.

4th

40th

42nd

44th

44th

48th

54th

56th Armd

17th Gurkha

17th British

1st Commonwealth

Training Brigade Groups

Home Counties

Lancastrian

Midland

East Anglian

Wessex

Yorks & Northumberland

Mercian

Welsh

North Irish

Greenjackets

PLATE 12

FORMATION SIGNS

Brigades

1st Guards

2nd Guards

2nd

3rd

5th

6th

8th

H.Q. 12th

12th

17th

18th

19th

22nd Beach

23rd

25th Armd

25th

27th

29th

30th Armd

31st

39th

39th

49th

50th

51st

72nd

107th

155th

160th

161st

162nd

264th Beach

302nd

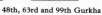

48th, 63rd and 99th Gurkha

PLATE 13

FORMATION SIGNS

British Forces Overseas

H.Q. Middle East
Land Forces

G.H.Q. Middle East
Land Forces

H.Q. Br. Troops
in Egypt

G.H.Q. Far East
Land Forces

Br. Troops
in Siam

Br. Troops
in Palestine

Malaya
Command

Persia and Iraq
Command

H.Q. Land Forces
Hong Kong

H.Q. Director of
Borneo Operations

Br. Troops
in Norway

Netherlands
District

Cyprus
District

BETFOR

Tripolitania
District

Cyrenaica
District

Singapore
District

Faroe Island
Force

North Palestine
District

Canal South
Distr. M.E.L.F.

H.Q. Br. Troops
in Aden

Land Forces
Adriatic

H.Q. B.C.O.F.
Japan-Korea

Allied Commn
Austria

Control Commn
Germany

Br. Troops
in France

Hamburg
District

Hanover
District

Br. Troops
in Berlin

H.Q. B.A.O.R.

Rhine Army
Troops

Rhine Army
Trng Centre

Sch. of Art
B.A.O.R.

Eng. Trng
Establ. B.A.O.R.

R.A.C. Trng
Centre B.A.O.R.

PLATE 14

Army Groups, R.A.

1st   2nd   3rd   5th   6th   7th

41st   42nd   84th   85th   86th   87th   88th

89th   90th   91st   92nd   93rd   94th   95th

96th   97th   98th   99th   100th   Maritime A.A.Art.

18th Trng Bde

1st Coast Art Trng School

Coast Brigades, R.A.

101st   102nd

Guided Weapons Regt

A.A. and Coast Defence (C.M.F.)

Coast Art. Trng Centre, S.W. Distr.

Coast Art. School

105th

Coast Artillery

A.A. Brigades, R.A.

30th   31st   33rd   34th

PLATE 15

FORMATION SIGNS
Engineer Groups

21st

22nd

23rd

24th

24th

25th

26th

27th

29th

Port Task Forces, R.E.

R.E. Base Group
Singapore

1st

2nd

3rd

R.E. Trng Bde

Transportation
Trng Centre R.E.

Bomb Disposal

Airfield Constr.
Groups, R.E.

Chem. Warfare

R.E. Depot

Miscellanea

R.A.C. Trng Bde

The War Office

Mil. Staff
Ministry of Supply

W.O. Controlled
units

Sigs Trng Regt

Sch. of Infantry

A.A.C.

Beach Groups

Special Trng
Centre

Air Despatch
Group

Air Formation Sigs

Army Dept Fleet

Air Liaison Sigs

PLATE 16

CAP BADGES

1st pattern   2nd pattern

Marshal of Poland and Generals

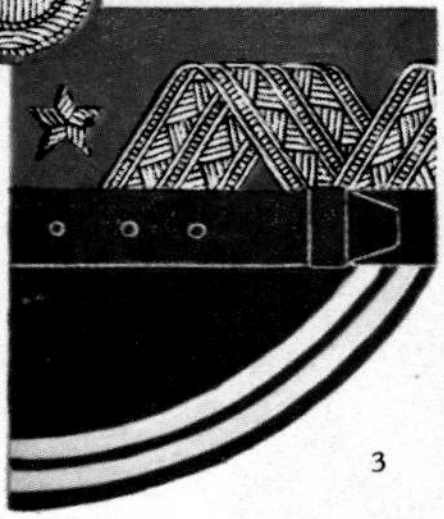

Senior Officers

Junior Officers

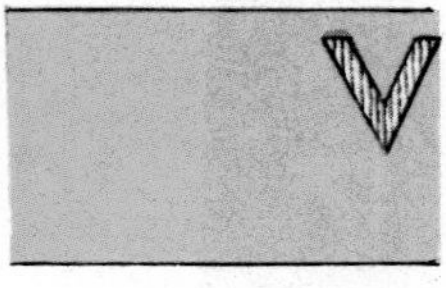

Other Ranks

PLATE 17

OFFICERS' RANK BADGES

| Marshal of Poland | General of Army | General | General of Division | General of Brigade |

| Colonel | Lieutenant-Colonel | Major |

| Captain | Lieutenant | 2nd Lieutenant | W.O. |

PLATE 18

WARRANT OFFICERS' AND N.C.O.s' RANK BADGES (1st pattern)

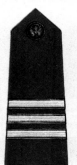

Staff Sergeant · Sergeant · Lance-Sergeant · Corporal · Lance-Corporal

(2nd pattern)

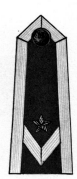

Senior Staff W.O. · Staff W.O. · Senior W.O. · W.O. · Junior W.O.

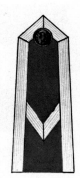

Senior Staff Sergeant · Staff Sergeant · Senior Sergeant · Sergeant

PLATE 19

RANK BADGES

| Platoon Sergeant | Senior Corporal | Corporal | Lance-Corporal |

COLLAR PATCHES (1949–52)

General – Infantry   Officer – Artillery

Engineers   Signals   Legal Service   Quartermaster Service

Administrative Service   Medical Service   Veterinaries   Mot. Transport Service

PLATE 20

COLLAR PATCHES FOR MARSHAL OF POLAND AND GENERALS (1952-60)

Armd/Mech. units   Warsaw Inf. Div.   Marshal of Poland   Generals–Inf.   Artillery   Eng./Mot. Transp.

Signals   Q.M. Admin.   Medical Service   Veterinaries   Legal Service

COLLAR PATCHES FOR OFFICERS AND OTHER RANKS (1952-60)

Chemical   Armd/Mech. units   Officers' Schools

Army   Armour

COLLAR BADGES

Infantry   Artillery   Armd/Mechanised   Signals   Ordnance   Pontoon units

Engineers   Chemical   Legal   Mot. Transport   Administrative   Q.M.

Construction Bns   Band   Mil. Railways   Medical   Veterinaries

PLATE 21

COLLAR BADGES (1961-73)

Marshal

Generals

Ordnance

Chemical

Infantry

Artillery

Engineers

Armour

Mech. units

Radiotechnical

Mot. Transport

Construction

Geographers

Mil. Transport

Signals

Administrative

Medical

Q.M.

Army Security

Legal

Veterinaries

Chaplains

Mountain Troops

Army Tech. Ac.

Army Med. Ac.

Officers Schools

N.C.O.s' Schools

SHOULDER-STRAP BADGES

Army Courses
in higher schools

W.O.s' School

Army Med. Ac.

Staff College

Army Tech. Ac.

Reg. N.C.O.s' School

PLATE 22

BREAST-POCKET BADGES FOR EXEMPLARY SERVICE

Exemplary Service

Rifleman

Light M.-Gunner

Reconnaissance

Driver

Marksman

Mortarman

Heavy M.-Gunner

Med. Orderly

Tankman

Sapper

Pontooner

Artilleryman

Cook

Baker

Miner

Exemplary Driver (3 classes)

ARM BADGES

Marines

Coastal Defence

N.C.O.s' School

PLATE 23

BREAST BADGES

1st Warsaw Inf. Div.

Grunwald badge

Frontier Defence

1st Warsaw
Cav. Div.

Inf. Trng Centre

Officers' Schools (12)

Inf. Officers'
School

Reg. N.C.O.s' School

Art. Off. School No. 1

Driver-Mech.

2nd Mot. Transp.
Trng Regt

13th
International Bde

Armd Corps

Youth Club

Parachutist

Inventiveness
Improvement

Exemplary Soldiers

Brotherhood of Arms

Driver-Mech. (Armour)

Officers' Schools and Academies

PLATE 24

ARM BADGES

6th POMORSKA Airborne Division

Specialists

| Armour | Artillery | A.A. Defence | Ordnance |

Mil. Transport   Topographer   Diver   Motor Transport   Quartermaster

Educational   Engineers   Chemical   Signals   Radiotechnical

PLATE 25

U.S.A.

CAP BADGES

Warrant Officers

Enlisted Men

Generals – Field Officers   Officers – Warrant Officers

Special Forces

SPECIAL FORCES INSIGNIA

J. F. Kennedy
S.W.C.

1st   3rd   5th   6th

7th   8th   10th   11th   19th   46th

S.W.C.   Europe   Reserve   Trng   5th Combas   Arctic Rangers   Avn

PLATE 26

OFFICERS' RANK BADGES

General of the Army   General   Lieutenant General   Major General   Brigadier

Colonel   Lieutenant Colonel   Major   Captain

1st Lieutenant   2nd Lieutenant

WARRANT OFFICERS' RANK BADGES

CWO4   CWO3   CWO2   WO1   CWO4   CWO3   CWO2   WO1

SHOULDER ORNAMENTATION FOR ARMY BLUE UNIFORM

Lieutenant General   Captain

Major

Colonel   CWO3

PLATE 27

LINE N.C.O.s' RANK BADGES (1948)

First Sergeant

Master Sergeant

Sergeant 1st Class

Sergeant

Corporal

Private 1st Class

(1955)

First Sergeant

Master Sergeant

Sergeant 1st Class

Sergeant

Corporal

Private 1st Class

(1957–73)

Command Sgt Major

Sergeant Major

First Sergeant

Master Sergeant

Sergeant 1st Class

Staff Sergeant

Sergeant

Corporal

Private 1st Class

Private E-2

PLATE 28

SPECIALISTS' RANK BADGES (1956)

| Master Specialist | Sp. 1st Class | Sp. 2nd Class | Sp. 3rd Class |

(1958)

Sp. 9   Sp. 8   Sp. 7   Sp. 6   Sp. 5   Sp. 4

SHOULDER SLEEVE TABS

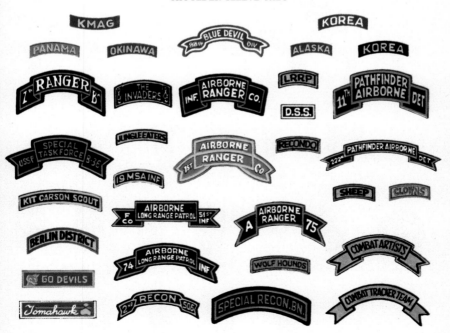

PLATE 29

OFFICERS' COLLAR BADGES

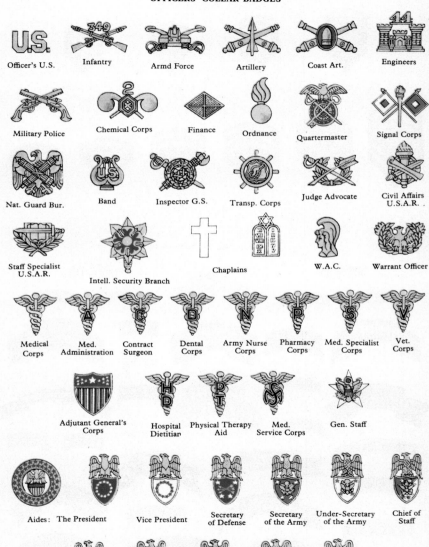

Officer's U.S.   Infantry   Armd Force   Artillery   Coast Art.   Engineers

Military Police   Chemical Corps   Finance   Ordnance   Quartermaster   Signal Corps

Nat. Guard Bur.   Band   Inspector G.S.   Transp. Corps   Judge Advocate   Civil Affairs U.S.A.R.

Staff Specialist U.S.A.R.   Intell. Security Branch   Chaplains   W.A.C.   Warrant Officer

Medical Corps   Med. Administration   Contract Surgeon   Dental Corps   Army Nurse Corps   Pharmacy Corps   Med. Specialist Corps   Vet. Corps

Adjutant General's Corps   Hospital Dietitian   Physical Therapy Aid   Med. Service Corps   Gen. Staff

Aides: The President   Vice President   Secretary of Defense   Secretary of the Army   Under-Secretary of the Army   Chief of Staff

to General of the Army   General   Lieutenant General   Major General   Brigadier General

PLATE 30

BREAST BADGES

Dept of Defense

White House
Service

Joint Chiefs
of Staff

General Staff

Honor Guard

Combat Infantryman

Expert Infantryman

C.I. 2nd Award

C.I. 3rd Award

Combat Field Artillery

Combat Armd Cavalry

Parachutist

Senior Para

Rigger

Master Para

Para Ranger

Glider

Nuclear Reactor
Operator, 1st Cl.

Senior Army
Aviator

Master Army
Aviator

Explosive Ordnance
Disposal

Exp. Ord. Disp.
Supervisor

Flight Surgeon

Expert Field
Medical

Combat Medical

C.M. 2nd Award

C.M. 3rd Award

C.M. 4th Award

PLATE 31

SHOULDER SLEEVE AND POCKET INSIGNIA

Recruiting and Training

F.A. School

Inf. School

Armed Forces
Information School

Army Avn
School

Air Def. School

V.N. Basic Trng
Center

U.S.A.R.S.

Special Warfare
Center

J.W.T.C.

Centers and Schools

F.A.

Missile and
Munitions

Signals

Q.M.

Transp.

M.P.

Ordnance

Helicopter School

Medical

Engr

Intelligence

Chemical

Combat Leadership
Trainee

Combat Surv.
Electr. School

Civil Affairs
School

Recondo Schools

G/75 Inf.

Judge Advocate
General's School

A.C.T.A.
2nd Div.

Command-G.S. College

Hawaii

U.S. Military Academy

5th Div.

54th Engr Professional
School

PLATE 32

SHOULDER SLEEVE AND POCKET INSIGNIA

U.S. Forces Overseas

Berlin Bde

Berlin District

Eur. Civil Affairs

Constabulary in Europe

U.S. Army Europe

Eur. Hqs E.T.O.

Tactical Cmd Austria

U.S. Forces Austria

Trieste U.S. Troops

U.S. Forces Far East

U.S.–Allied Control Commn–Hungary

Med. Cmd Europe

Guam Base

Ryukus Cmd

Japan Log. Cmd

West Pacific Far East Cmd

Military Government Korea

Japanese War Crimes Trial

Nurenberg District

U.S. TASCOM Europe

Communications Zone Korea

MAAG Laos

MAAG Taiwan

U.S. Army Missions

Civil Assistance Commn Korea

U.N. Partisan Force Korea

Engr Cmd Europe

Mil. Equipment Delivery Team Cambodia

Mil. Asst. Cmd V.N.

U.S. Army V.N.

Engr Cmd V.N.

1st Field Force   2nd Field Force

PLATE 33

SHOULDER SLEEVE AND POCKET INSIGNIA
Miscellaneous U.S. Units

China Hqs

Ledo Road

Marshall Task Force

Bushmasters
158th Regt Comb.

480th F.A.

Katchin

Jingpaw

Rangers

O.S.S.–Special Force

99th Inf. Bn.

36th Engr Bn

2nd Cml
M. Bn

83rd Cml M. Bn

Office of
Strategic Services

49th A.A. Bde

98th F.A. Bn

1629th Engr Bn

93rd Cml M. Bn.

96th Cml M. Bn

Trng Engr

Engr Intell. Dept

Combat
Development

Guided Missile
Agency

Q.M.

SCARWAF

Security Agency

Army Avn Team

Defense Atomic
Support Agency

Manhattan
Project

Arctic Test Center

Sp. Forces Avn

1st Avn Bn Flight Sect.

Alaska Supply Group

Arctic Rangers

100th Cml M. Bn

Special Forces

Pathfinders

Alaska Cmd

PLATE 34

SHOULDER SLEEVE INSIGNIA

Ghost Units

1st Army Group

14th Army

31st Army Corps

33rd Army Corps

11th Div.

14th Div.

17th Div.

22nd Div.

46th Div.

48th Div.

50th Div.

55th Div.

59th Div.

108th Div.

119th Div.

130th Div.

141st Div.

157th Div.

National Guard Divisions

46th

47th

48th

49th

51st

Miscellanea

1st Army

2nd Army

19th Army Corps

5th Div.

40th Div.

89th Div.

11th Air Assault Div. (Test)

PLATE 35

U.S.A.

SHOULDER SLEEVE INSIGNIA
Regimental Combat Teams

4th

5th

25th

29th

33rd

38th

75th

103rd

107th

111th

150th

157th

158th

163rd

166th

176th

178th

182nd

187th Abn

196th

278th

295th

296th

298th

299th

351st

442nd

474th

508th Abn

99th Bn C.T.

187th Abn

65th

442nd (1st)

PLATE 36

SHOULDER SLEEVE INSIGNIA
Brigades

1st Inf.	2nd Inf.	11th Inf.	29th Inf.	32nd Inf.	33rd Inf.	36th Inf.

39th Inf.	40th Inf.	40th Armd	41st Inf.	45th Inf.	49th Inf.	49th Armd

53rd Inf.	67th Inf.	69th Inf.	71st Abn	72nd Inf.	81st Inf.	86th Armd

92nd Inf.	157th Inf.	171st Inf.	172nd Inf.	173rd Abn	187th Inf.	191st Inf.

193rd Inf.	194th Armd	196th Inf.	197th Inf.	198th Inf.	199th Inf.	205th Inf.

256th Inf.	30th Art.	31st, 35th, 45th 47th, 49th, 52nd ARADCOM	32nd Air Defense	38th Art.	40th AA	107th Art.

PLATE 37

SHOULDER SLEEVE INSIGNIA
Brigades

7th Engr   16th Engr   18th Engr   20th Engr   130th Engr   411th Engr   412th Engr

416th Engr   420th Engr   57th Ordnance   1st Signal   7th Signal

1st Spt   2nd Spt   3rd Spt   12th Spt   13th Spt

15th Spt   35th Spt   103rd Spt   167th Spt   301st Spt   311th Spt   377th Spt

15th M.P.   18th M.P.   43rd M.P.   220th M.P.   221st M.P.   258th M.P.   290th M.P.

7th Med.   18th Med.   44th Med.   1st Avn   107th Tpn   125th Tpn   143rd Tpn

PLATE 38

SHOULDER SLEEVE INSIGNIA
Logistical Commands

1st

2nd

3rd

4th

5th

7th

8th

9th

300th

304th

305th

306th

307th

310th

312th

313th

315th

316th

319th

321st

322nd

323rd

324th

Transportation Commands

2nd

3rd

4th

5th

7th

11th

32nd

124th

184th

425th

PLATE 39

SHOULDER SLEEVE AND POCKET INSIGNIA
Commands

14th A.A.

Air Defense

Army Material

Special Amm. Support

Army Missile

300th M.P.–P.W.

Criminal Investigation

1st, 261st Signal

7th, 8th, 22nd, 23rd FASCOMs

Cavalry–Armoured and Airmobile

150th A.C.R.

F.A. Bde 1st Div.

29th Art. Regt

6th C.R.

17th Cav. Recon.

3rd A.C.R.

2nd A.C.R.

4th C. Group

14th A.C.R.

15th C. Group

6th C. Group

A/1st/9th

11th A.C.R.

101st A.C.R.

A/4th/12th A.C.R.

Heli. Medical Evacuation

C.M.P.P.

107th A.C.R.

163rd A.C.R.

PLATE 40

SHOULDER SLEEVE AND POCKET INSIGNIA

Armored Force

Hqs

3rd Armd Corps

1st Armd Div.

325th Armd Bn

The Armored Center

G.H.Q.

1st Armd Div.

3rd Armd Div. Reconnaissance

30th Armd Div. N.G.

112th Armd Cav.

7th Cav. Regt

Demonstration Regt

7th Army Tank Training Center

17th Armd Group

510th Armd Reconnaissance Bn

Tank Co. 39th Inf.

522nd Armd Engr Bn

1st Bn, 151st Armor

Special Airborne Training Unit

70th Armd Regt

T.C.Q.C. Grafenwohr

628th Tank Destr. Bn

PLATE 41

SHOULDER SLEEVE AND POCKET INSIGNIA

Para. Glider, Abn Infantry, Glider Infantry and Para. Infantry Regts

187th P.G.I.   187th A.I.R.   Mortar Btry 187th   188th A.I.R.

188th A.I.R.   1st Bat. Gp 325th   325th G.I.R.   Recon. Pl. 327th   501st P.I.R.

501st P.I.R.   502nd P.I.R.   503rd P.I.R.

503rd P.I.R.   504th P.I.R.   505th P.I.R.

H.G. 505th   506th P.I.R.   507th P.I.R.   508th P.I.R.   509th P.I.R.

509th P.I.R.   Recon. Pl. 509th   509th P.I.R.   511th A.I.R.

PLATE 42

SHOULDER SLEEVE AND POCKET INSIGNIA

Airborne and Parachute Infantry Regts and Miscellaneous Para. Units

511th A.I.R.

511th P.I.R.

513th P.I.R.

515th P.I.R.

517th P.I.R.

541st P.I.R.

542nd P.I.R.

550th P.I.R.

551st P.I.R.

555th P.I.R.

127th Abn Engr

Abn Eng (W.W.2)

460th Para F. A. Bn

674th P.F.A. Bn

307th Injuneers

370th Abn Engr

596th Abn Engr

462nd P.F.A. Bn

Aerial Supply

Abn School
Ft Benning

AIRBORNE

U.S. ARMY PARACHUTE TEAM

GOLDEN KNIGHTS

Aerial Supply

50th Abn Sig. Bn

Allied Forces Abn
Trng Center (W.W.2)

SEVENTH ARMY PARACHUTE TEAM

Parachute Teams

PLATE 43

SHOULDER SLEEVE AND POCKET INSIGNIA
Airborne Divisions (O.R.)

1st/225th Inf. Regt

80th

84th

100th

108th

Ghost Airborne Divisions

6th

9th

18th

21st

135th

Airborne Brigades and Other Units

2nd

173rd

24th Inf.

187th A.I.R.
503rd A.I.R.

509th A.I.R.

2nd Field Force

82nd and 101st Airborne Divisions

Command and Control
82nd

82nd

VIETNAM

VIETNAM

101st

101st Abn Div. at
Ft Campbell

Intell. Det.
82nd

Sig. Bn
82nd

Divisional Recondos

Spt Cmd
101st

101st Abn Div
Reunion

7th Ranger Bn

PLATE 44

CAP INSIGNIA

General of Army Corps
A.C. General with Special Appointments

Other Generals

Cap bands and chinstraps

All officers

W.O.s and N.C.O.s

Generals

Senior Officers

Junior Officers

Warrant Officers

Rank badges worn on the field cap

Generals

Senior Officers

Junior Officers

Warrant Officers

Mountain Troops

Officers' feather holders

Rank badge (Major)

O.R.s' feather holders

PLATE 45

OFFICERS' AND WARRANT OFFICERS' RANK BADGES

A. C. General with Special Appointments   General of Army Corps   General of Division   General of Brigade

Colonel   Lieutenant-Colonel   Major   Captain   Lieutenant   2nd Lieutenant

Aiutante di battaglia   W.O. Major   Chief W.O.   W.O.

PLATE 46

OFFICERS' RANK BADGES (BLACK UNIFORM)

1st pattern

Generals

Senior Officers

Junior Officers

2nd pattern

Generals

Senior Officers

Junior Officers

SERGEANTS AND CORPORALS

Sergeant-Major

Sergeant

Corporal-Major

Corporal

CADETS

Officer

N.C.O.

Squad Commander

PLATE 47

CAP BADGES

Infantry

Inf. Folgore Div.

Bersaglieri

Lagunari

Grenadiers

Parachutists

Tanks

Lancers

Dragoons

Cavalry

Heavy Artillery

Medium Artillery

Field Artillery

Missile Artillery

Horse Artillery

Armoured Artillery

A.A. Artillery

Heavy A.A. Artillery

Art. Folgore Div

Terr. Air Defence

Engineers

Signals

PLATE 48

CAP BADGES

Railway Eng.

Miners

Bridging Eng.

Pionieri d'Arresto

Chaplains

Doctors

Pharmacists

Veterinaries

Motor Transport

Clerks

Administrative Service

Medical Service

Supply Service

N.B.C.

Commissaries

Technical Services

Legal Service

Fencing Instructors

Armd Troops
Training School

Military Academy

Military Schools

Military Postal Service

PLATE 49

MOUNTAIN TROOPS' CAP BADGES

Artillery

Engineers

Administrative

Alpini

Supply

Motor Transport

Medical

Signals

Commissaries

Doctors

Veterinaries

Chaplains

Pharmacists

O.R.s

ENAMEL BADGES

PLATE 50

ITALY

COLLAR PATCHES

Grenadiers

Infantry

Mortars

Frontier Guards

Unassigned Infantry

Bersaglieri

Alpini

Tanks

Cavalry Depot

1st Nizza Cav. Regt

2nd Piemonte

3rd Gorizia

3rd Savoia

4th Genova

5th Novara

6th Aosta

7th Milano

8th Montebello

12th Saluzzo

14th Alessandria

15th Lodi

19th Guide

N.B.C.

Artillery

Engineers

Medical

Veterinaries

Commissaries

Supply

Administrative

Signals

Clerks

Fencing Instructors

Armd Infantry

Motor Transport

PLATE 51

ITALY

COLLAR PATCHES

Mountain Troops

Armoured Troops

Parachutists

Parachutists

Folgore Inf. Division

Technical Services

Artillery

Engineers

Chemical

Geographical

Signals

Motor Transport

PLATE 52

Parachutists

Military Parachute Centre

Arm badges (1940–64)

Veterans
Folgore Div.

Air Supply

Breast badges (1964)

Para. Guastatore

Rigger

1st Tactical Group

Para. Artillery

Para. Saboteur

Lagunari

Breast badge

Collar patch

Cuff patch

PLATE 53

SPECIALISTS' BADGES

Metal Badges

Tank badges

Army Aviation Pilot

Anti-Tank

Motor-car and Motorcycle Drivers

Plastic Badges

Tank and Armd Car Crews   Fitter

Inf. Assault   Instructor Alpine School

Embroidered Badges

Guastatore   Artificer

Pioneer   Engine Driver

SPECIALISTS' ARM SHIELDS AND POCKET BADGES

PLATE 54

ARM SHIELDS

Infantry Divisions and Brigades

Folgore

Cremona

Legnano

Friuli

Mantova

Gran. di Sardegna

Aosta

Avellino

Pinerolo

Trieste

Armoured Divisions and Brigades

Ariete

Centauro

Somaliland
Security Corps

Pozzuolo del Friuli

Mountain Brigades

Taurineense

Julia

Tridentina

Orobica

Cadore

Miscellanea

Parachute Bde

Missile Bde

Garrison in Trieste

Frontier Guard

PLATE 55

TRAINING SCHOOLS' ARM SHIELDS

Electronic Def. Centre   Recr. Trng Centre   Armd Units Trng Camp

Mil. Riding School   N.C.O.s' School   War School   Army Avn Trng Centre   Mil. Medical School

Infantry   Signals   Mountain Troops   Engineers   Motor Transport

Army Sport Centre   Parachute   Veterinary   Commissariat, Admin. and Supply   Mil. Phys. Trng Schoo

Armoured Troops   Art. Electronic Technicians   Artillery   A.A. Artillery

PLATE 56

CAP BADGES

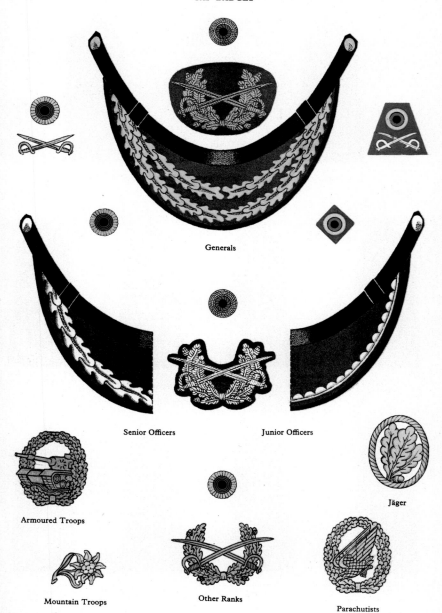

Generals

Senior Officers   Junior Officers

Armoured Troops

Mountain Troops

Other Ranks

Jäger

Parachutists

PLATE 57

OFFICERS' RANK BADGES (1955–62)

Lieutenant-General   Major-General   Brigadier-General

Colonel   Colonel   Lieutenant-Colonel   Major
(1955–56)

Captain   Captain   1st Lieutenant   Lieutenant
(1955–56)

PLATE 58

N.C.O.s' RANK BADGES (1955–57)

Oberstabsfeldwebel

Stabsfeldwebel

Oberfeldwebel

Feldwebel

Stabsunteroffizier

Hauptgefreiter

Obergefreiter

Unteroffizier

Gefreiter

(1957–59)

Oberstabsfeldwebel

Stabsfeldwebel

Hauptfeldwebel

Oberfeldwebel

Feldwebel

PLATE 59

OFFICERS' RANK BADGES (1962)

General

Lieutenant-General

Major-General

Brigadier-General

Colonel

Lieutenant-Colonel

Major

Captain

1st Lieutenant

Lieutenant

PLATE 60

N.C.O.s' RANK BADGES (1962–1964 pattern)

Oberstabsfeldwebel   Stabsfeldwebel   Hauptfeldwebel

Oberfeldwebel Feldwebel Stabsunteroffizier Unteroffizier

Hauptgefreiter   Obergefreiter   Gefreiter   Obergefreiter (1972)

PLATE 61

G.F.R.

OFFICER CADETS

Fähnrich

Oberfähnrich

Fähnrich

Fahnenjunker

Gefreiter OA

Officer Cadet star

Gefreiter UA

N.C.O. CADETS

FIELD UNIFORM RANK BADGES

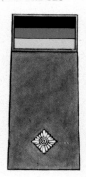

PLATE 62

COLLAR BADGES

Infantry

Armour

Artillery

Signals

Anti-Tank

Anti-Aircraft

Engineers

Chemical

Ordnance

Medical

Quartermasters

M.P.

Band

Army Aviation

MISCELLANEOUS INSIGNIA

Belt buckle

Mountain Troops

Parachutists

Marksman's lanyard

Mountain Guide

Single-Handed Combat

PLATE 63

COLLAR PATCHES

Generals

G.S. Service

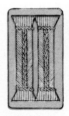

Infantry   Armour   Armd Reconnaissance   Artillery   Army A.A.

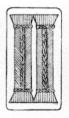

Engineers   Signals   Army Aviation   Band   M.P.   A.B.C. Defenc

Technical Troops   Medical   Armd Infantry   Anti-Tank   Quartermasters

PLATE 64

PARACHUTISTS' WINGS

1

2

3

ARM BADGES

Medical

Pharmacists

Veterinaries

Dentists

Geographical

Storekeeper

Radio Operator

Book-keeper

Artificer

Repair Maintenance
Fitter

Radar
Fire Control

Helmsman

Diver

Fortification
Maintenance

Equipment
Inspector

Rigger

Air Protection

CUFF TITLES

Guard Battalion

Army Aviation

PLATE 65

FORMATION BADGES

Ministry of Defence

Military District
Command

H.Q. Corps and
Corps Troops

Depot

1st Armd Inf. Div.

2nd Armd Inf. Div.
(now Rifle Div.)

3rd Armd Div.

4th Armd Inf. Div.
(now Rifle Div.)

5th Armd Div.

6th Armd Inf. Div.

7th Armd Inf. Div.

1st Mountain Div.

1st Airborne Div.

10th Armd Inf. Div.
(now Armd Div.)

11th Armd Inf. Div.

12th Armd Div.

PLATE 66

CAP BADGES

Generals—Army

Officers—Border Troops

Other Ranks

BREAST BADGES

G.S. Academy
of the
Soviet Army

Military Academy
F. Engels

Mil. Medical Section
E.-M. Arndt University

Graduate
Officers

Military Academy
of the
Soviet Army

Exemplary Soldier

Proficiency
Army

Proficiency
Border Troops

Military Sports

Parachutist

PLATE 67

OFFICERS' RANK BADGES

General of Army Colonel-General Lieutenant-General Major-General

Colonel Lieutenant-Colonel Major

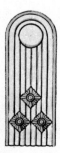

Captain 1st Lieutenant Lieutenant 2nd Lieutenant

PLATE 68

N.C.O.s' RANK BADGES

Stabsfeldwebel

Oberfeldwebel

Feldwebel

Unterfeldwebel

Unteroffizier

Stabsgefreiter

Gefreiter

Bandsman

CADETS' RANK BADGES

SERVICE STRIPES

Officers' School

N.C.O.s' School

1st pattern

2nd pattern

PLATE 69

PATCHES/ARM-OF-SERVICE COLOURS

Generals' Collar and Cuff Patches

Army   Border Troops

Officers' Collar Patches

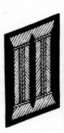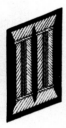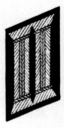

Infantry   Artillery   Armour   Services   Signals

Officers' and Other Ranks' Cuff Patches–O.R.s' Collar Patches

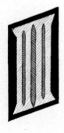

Engineers
Techn. Troops   Border Troops   Parachutists   Pioneers   Air Defence

PLATE 70

MISCELLANEOUS INSIGNIA

Proficiency Badges

All Arms

Armour

Qualification Badges

Tank Driver, 1st Class

Driver, 3rd Class

Signaller, 1st Class

Diver, 1st Class

Marksman's Lanyard

Infantry, Artillery and Armour

Belt Buckles

Officers

Other Ranks

PLATE 71

ARM BADGES

General Services

Chemical   Signals   Radio Location   Storekeeper

Motor-Driver Tech. Service   Artificer   Radiotechnical   Medical   Legal   Information

Army Services

Armour   Artillery   Pioneer

Mil. Transportation   Armour Tech. Service   Artillery Ordnance   H.Q. Messenger   Reconnaissance

Border Troops

Chief Dog Handler   Diver   Pioneer   Ordnance

PLATE 72

SERVICE CHEVRONS (26.11.1945)

SHOULDER BOARDS (31.1.1947)

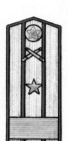

Generals and Officers on the Reserve List

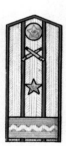

Generals and Officers on the Retired List

ARM BADGES

Parachutists (18.8.1947)   Railway Military Transport (13.2.1951)

PLATE 73

Railway Military Transport (13.2.1951)

SERVICE CHEVRONS (31.3.1952)

LAPELS OF PARADE AND ORDINARY UNIFORMS (9.4.1954)

Marshal of the Soviet Union   Supreme Marshals, Marshals and Generals

CUFFS OF PARADE UNIFORMS

PLATE 74

LAPELS AND CUFFS

Ordinary Uniforms (10.6.1954)   **Parade and Ordinary Uniforms (25.2.1955)**

Marshal
of the Soviet Union

Other Marshals
and Generals

Officers

VISORS AND CHINSTRAPS (10.6.1954)

All Marshals and Generals

Officers

BELTS (25.2.1955)

All Marshals and Generals

Officers

PLATE 75

PARADE PEAKED CAPS (1955)

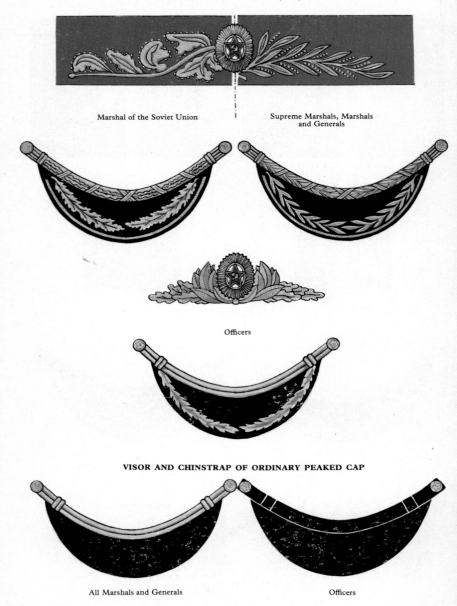

Marshal of the Soviet Union

Supreme Marshals, Marshals
and Generals

Officers

VISOR AND CHINSTRAP OF ORDINARY PEAKED CAP

All Marshals and Generals

Officers

PLATE 76

ARM-OF-SERVICE BADGES (1955)

Mot. Rifle units

Parachutists

Artillery

Armour

Commissariat
Administrative

Engineers
Tech. Troops

Signals

Medical

Veterinary

Railway
Mil. Transport

Mot. Transport

Topographical

Tech. Troops

Legal

Pioneers

Band

COLLAR PATCHES FOR OVERCOAT (23.6.1955)

Marshal of the Soviet Union, Supreme Marshals, Marshals and Generals

Marshal of the Soviet Union

Medical–Veterinary

Legal

Mot. Rifle units

Artillery–Armour

Technical–Commissariat

Officers

Mot. Rifle units
Commissariat–Legal

Artillery–Armour
Technical Troops

Medical–Veterinary
Administrative

PLATE 77

Orchestra of the Regimental Garrison at Moscow (11.3.1955)

Officer and Soldier of the Honorary Guards (1.8.1955)

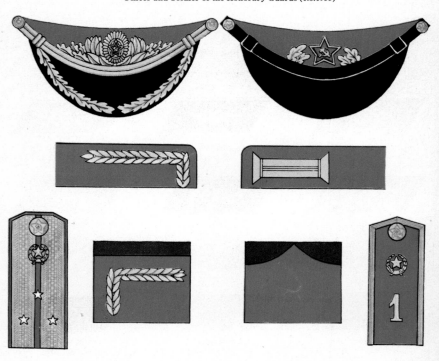

PLATE 78

OFFICERS' RANK BADGES

Parade and Walking-Out Uniforms (22.9.1956)

Marshal of the Soviet Union

Supreme Marshals

Marshals

29.3.1958

General of Army

Colonel-General

Lieutenant-General

Major-General

Colonel

Lieutenant-Colonel

Major

PLATE 79

U.S.S.R.

OFFICERS' RANK BADGES

Parade and Walking-Out Uniform (29.3.1958)

Captain

Senior Lieutenant

Lieutenant

Junior Lieutenant

Ordinary Uniform

Marshal
of the Soviet Union

Supreme Marshals

Marshals

Colonel-General

Lieutenant-Colonel

Senior Lieutenant

PLATE 80

OFFICERS' RANK BADGES

Field Uniform (29.3.1958)

All Marshals, Generals and Officers

N.C.O.s' RANK BADGES

Parade/Walking-Out and Ordinary/Field Uniforms (30.12.1955)

| Sergeant-Major | Senior Sergeant | Sergeant | Junior Sergeant | Corporal |

29.3.1958

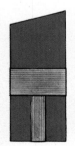   

| Parade/Walking-Out | Ordinary | Field Uniform |

PLATE 81

CAP BADGES AND LAPELS (29.3.1958)

Ordinary

Parade/Walking-Out

Field

Ordinary Uniforms **Parade and Ordinary Uniforms**

Marshal
of the Soviet Union

Other Marshals
and Generals

Officers

SHOULDER BOARDS AND SERVICE CHEVRONS

after 1 year

after 2 years

after 3 years

Sergeant-Major
(1963)

Warrant Officer
(1.1.1972)

after 4 years

after 5–9 years

after 10 years and over

BREAST BADGES

Inf. Specialist

Extended Service

Tank crew

Proficiency

PLATE 82

ARM BADGES

Traffic Controller

Mot. Rifle units

Airborne

Other Ranks
(Shoulder Strap)

Armour

Artillery

Signals

Engineers

Chemical

Railway Mil. Transport

Motor Transport

Pipeline Troops

Construction Troops

Medical/Veterinaries

Band

PLATE 83

GENERALS' AND SENIOR OFFICERS' RANK BADGES

Generals

Lieutenant-General

Major-General

Brigadier-General

Colonel-Brigadier

Senior Officers

Colonel

Lieutenant-Colonel

Major

PLATE 84

JUNIOR OFFICERS' AND WARRANT OFFICERS' RANK BADGES

Junior Officers

1st Captain

Captain

Lieutenant

2nd Lieutenant

W.O. 1st Class

Warrant Officers

W.O.

OTHER COLLAR PATCHES

Advocate Generals

Judge Advocates

Ingénieurs des
Fabrications Militaires
(Lieutenant-Colonel)

Clerks

Medical Service
(O.R.)

PLATE 85

BELGIUM

SERGEANTS' AND CORPORALS' RANK BADGES

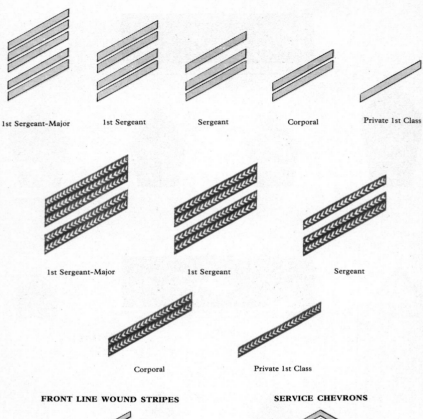

1st Sergeant-Major 1st Sergeant Sergeant Corporal Private 1st Class

1st Sergeant-Major 1st Sergeant Sergeant

Corporal Private 1st Class

FRONT LINE WOUND STRIPES   **SERVICE CHEVRONS**

ARMLETS

Military Police   Regimental Police

PLATE 86

Royal Military School's Shoulder Cords and Badges

| 1st year | 2nd year | 3rd year | 4th year | 5th year |

Cadet

Instructor

Polytechnic

Arm-of-Service Schools

Wings

Parachutist

Commandos Trng Centre

Parachute Instructor

S.A.S.

Bde Schools and Graduates

N.C.O.s' School

Para-Commando

P.T. Instructors

PLATE 87

FORMATION SIGNS

Ground Forces Base

1st Army Corps

2nd

Airborne

Home Defence
Forces

Commandos

1st Inf. Division   2nd Inf. Division   3rd Inf. Division   4th Inf. Division   5th Inf. Division   16th Armd Division

ARM-OF-SERVICE BADGES

Generals   General Staff   Commissaries   Advocate Generals   Judge Advocates

Medical, Veterinary
and Pharmacist Officers

Protestant, Catholic and Jewish Chaplains

Ingénieurs des
Fabrications Militaires

PLATE 88

ARM-OF-SERVICE BADGES

Carabiniers

Chasseurs-on-Foot

Grenadiers

Chasseurs of
the Ardennes

Training Centre

Parachutists

Infantry

M.P.

Base Personnel

'Liberation' Bn

Commandos

Guides

Engineers

Chasseurs-on-Horse

Security

Armd Troops School

Pioneers

Lancers

Royal Mil. School

Artillery

Military Railways

R.A.S.C.

R.A.O.C.

Band

Belgian Lion

R.E.M.E.

PLATE 89

ARM-OF-SERVICE BADGES

Trumpeters

Logistical Corps

Med. Vet. Pharm.
Service (O.R.s)

Legal Service
Clerks

Administrative Service

Tank Bns (Inf. Divs)

SHOULDER-STRAP NUMERALS

BERET BADGES

R.A.S.C.

Artillery

Logistical Corps

R.E.M.E.

Engineers

Administrative

Signals (1st)

R.A.O.C.

Signals (2nd)

M.P.

Medical

Army Aviation

PLATE 90

BERET BADGES
Chasseurs-on-Horse

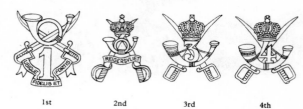

| 1st | 2nd | 3rd | 4th |

Guides

| 1st | 2nd | 3rd | 4th |

Lancers

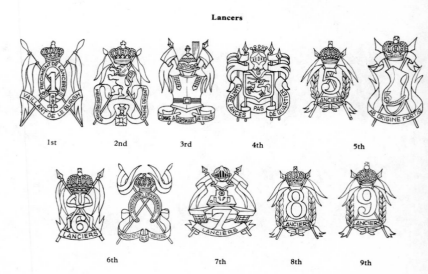

| 1st | 2nd | 3rd | 4th | 5th |

| 6th | 7th | 8th | 9th |

PLATE 91

BERET BADGES
Infantry

1st Infantry

2nd

3rd

4th

5th

6th

7th

8th

9th

11th

12th

13th

14th

Grenadiers

Mortar Coy

Chasseurs of the
Ardennes

1st Para.
Bn

2nd Commando
Bn

3rd Para.
Bn

Carabiniers

1st Chasseurs-on-
Foot

2nd

3rd

PLATE 92

BERET BADGES
Schools and Training

Royal Military School

Infantry School

Artillery School

Armoured School

Inf. Training Staff

Engineers School

Armd Troops Demonstration Det.

Armd Troops Trng Centre

Cadets School

Armoured Units

1st Heavy Tank Bn

1st Heavy Tank Bn

4th Heavy Tank Bn

Carabiniers

1st Recce Sq. (1–4)

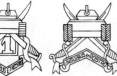

Recce Sqs

16th Armd Div.

Missile Coy (Inf. Bde)

PLATE 93

Great Britain

Great Britain was once one of the most powerful nations in the world but, as it was a colonial power, the major share of the glory usually went to the Royal Navy.

Armies were raised in time of trouble and hurriedly disbanded as soon as peace was restored. Later, the Standing Army was divided into two separate branches, the first consisting of regular soldiers, the second of territorials (militia, volunteers, yeomanry, etc.). In peacetime both regulars and territorials were, and still are, volunteers.

In 1902 a khaki service dress was adopted and the traditional coloured uniforms were finally discarded during World War 1, and during the following decades most armies of the world adopted khaki uniforms as well.

At the end of World War 2 the British soldier wore a khaki battledress which consisted of a beret (or helmet), a blouse and trousers tucked into anklets. The belts and anklets were made of woven 'webbing' material. The berets were khaki except for those of the armoured and airborne forces and the Commandos, who wore black, maroon and green berets respectively, and the 11th Hussars, who had a beret with a scarlet band.

The officers also wore the same battledress with a peaked cap, or a service dress composed of a peaked cap, jacket with open collar and four patch pockets and trousers.

Troops serving in hot climates had appropriate uniforms made of light materials, of a sandy-yellow colour.

National Service returned after the war in 1947 and lasted until 1960. During this period the battledress was considerably improved: dark blue berets were issued to the infantry and the collar of the blouse was opened up to show the shirt and tie. Collar badges were therefore re-adopted by most regiments and some coloured shoulder titles replaced the white and red ones previously used. For instance, the Essex Regiment adopted new ones with the word 'ESSEX' in yellow on a violet background, the Green Howards with white lettering on a green background and the North Staffordshire Regiment with white and black titles.

During 1961 and 1962 battledress was replaced by the new No. 2 dress, consisting of single-breasted belted jacket of khaki barathea, with four patch pockets and matching trousers, to be worn by officers and other ranks. A combat dress of disruptive-pattern camouflage material was introduced for certain units at the same time.

Plate 1. Officers' Rank Badges

The officers' ranks have not changed since the War and the rank badges also have remained the same, with the exception of the crown which, after the coronation of Elizabeth II in 1953, was changed to the St Edward's pattern.

Field-Marshals and generals wear crossed batons and crossed baton and sword respectively; generals with stars and crowns added for each rank. The batons and swords are also shown in the cap badge. The officers of field rank wear the crown, with additional stars; the subalterns only the stars.

Since the 1950s the officers' rank badges have also been made in anodised metal, although the previous gilded and embroidered patterns are still in use.

The chaplains of the Royal Army Chaplains' Department rank as follows: Chaplain-General – Major-General; Deputy Chaplain-General – Brigadier; Chaplain 1st Class – Colonel; Chaplain 2nd Class – Lieutenant-Colonel; Chaplain 3rd Class – Major; Chaplain 4th Class – Captain.

Warrant Officers' and N.C.O.s' Rank Badges

The basic ranks are those of Warrant Officers of First and Second Class, Staff Sergeant, Sergeant, Corporal and Lance-Corporal, and a number of appointment ranks are held as well.

The title of Corporal replaces that of Sergeant in the Household Cavalry which, together with the Brigade of Guards, has no one-chevron rank.

Four chevrons pointing upwards below a crown are worn on both fore-arms by Squadron Quartermaster-Corporals and Staff Corporals of the Household Cavalry while Pipe-Majors of the Brigade of Guards, and Drum-Majors, Pipe-Majors, Bugle-Majors, etc., wear a small drum, bagpipe and bugle above the four chevrons. The Master Gunners and Sergeants of the Royal Artillery wear a small gun together with their rank badges; the Sergeants of the Royal Engineers have a small grenade and those of the Royal Corps of Signals wear the figure of Mercury above their chevrons. A lyre is the badge of the bandsmen.

The brass badges of the Staff Sergeant-Major, Regimental Quarter-master-Sergeant and warrant officers, and also the brass crowns, guns, drums, etc. worn with chevrons, are currently made in anodised metal. Some smaller chevrons for summer wear are also made in anodised brass. Those of the Staff Sergeant have a small crown attached to the top.

During the war the N.C.O.s' chevrons used to be composed of individual stripes whilst now they are machine-embroidered in white cotton in one, two or more stripes on khaki felt. White cotton chevrons are used on summer uniforms.

Cap Badges

All British servicemen wear the badge of the corps, department or regiment they belong to on the head-dress. The officers' and other ranks' cap badges are usually similar, although the officers have badges made of superior metals, i.e. gilt and silver plate, instead of anodised metal, and some officers' badges are also embellished with coloured enamels. The first badges made of anodised aluminium were introduced in the early 1950s and soon became the official standard O.R.s' cap badges, replacing the old brass and white metal badges previously in use.

The officers of some corps and regiments wear embroidered cap badges on the forage cap or beret and some of these badges differ from the standard pattern used on the peaked cap. All the officers of the Gurkha battalions and Gurkha Engineers wear a small variation of their usual cap badge mounted on a coloured cord boss on the peaked cap, forage cap and beret. I have illustrated only the cap badges worn by other ranks, if not stated otherwise.

The badges of the Royal Artillery, Royal Armoured Corps, Royal Engineers and the other corps and services, schools, etc., have been grouped together under the title of Arms and Services. The following is the order of precedence of the corps, etc., of the British Army:

The Life Guards and the Blues
  and Royals
Royal Horse Artillery
Royal Armoured Corps
  (Armoured Cavalry Regiments)
Royal Tank Regiment
Royal Regiment of Artillery
Corps of Royal Engineers
Royal Corps of Signals
Regiment of Foot Guards
Regiments of Infantry
Special Air Service Regiment
Army Air Corps
Royal Army Chaplains'
  Department
Royal Corps of Transport
Royal Army Medical Corps
Royal Army Ordnance Corps

Corps of Royal Electrical and
  Mechanical Engineers
Corps of Royal Military Police
Royal Army Pay Corps
Royal Army Veterinary Corps
Small Arms School Corps
Military Provost Staff Corps
Royal Army Educational Corps
Royal Army Dental Corps
Royal Pioneer Corps
Intelligence Corps
Army Physical Training Corps
Army Catering Corps
General Service Corps
Queen Alexandra's Royal Army
  Nursing Corps
Women's Royal Army Corps

Plate 2. Cap Badges
Household Cavalry and Armoured Cavalry Regiments

The Royal Dragoons (1st Dragoons), known as the Royals, was the first cavalry regiment to change cap badge after World War 2. The new badge commemorated the capture of the standard of the 105th French Regiment at Waterloo and was used previously by the Royals before 1898 and unofficially during World War 1. Finally, in 1948, the French Eagle replaced the Royal Crest and was worn until 1969, when the Royals were merged with the Royal Horse Guards to form a new regiment, the Blues and Royals.

In 1953 the Household Cavalry (Life Guards and Royal Horse Guards badges and Household Cavalry badge with Garter, used by both regiments) adopted the St Edward's Crown and the cypher of Elizabeth II on their badges.

The 1st King's Dragoon Guards and the Queen's Bays (2nd Dragoon Guards) were amalgamated in 1959 to form the Queen's Dragoon Guards. The new regiment wears the old cap badge of the King's Dragoon Guards and the collar badges of the Bays, now with the new crown.

A new cap badge was also adopted by the Royal Scots Dragoon Guards (Carabiniers and Greys), a new regiment formed by merging the 3rd Carabiniers (Prince of Wales's Dragoon Guards) and the Royal Scots Greys (2nd Dragoons). In November 1958, the Queen's Own Hussars was formed by the amalgamation of the 3rd King's Own Hussars and the 7th Queen's Own Hussars while a month earlier the 4th Queen's Own Hussars and the 8th King's Royal Irish Hussars were reformed as the Queen's Royal Irish Hussars. Later, in 1969, the 10th Royal Hussars (Prince of Wales's Own) and the 11th Hussars (Prince Albert's Own) were also amalgamated into one regiment: the Royal Hussars (Prince of Wales's Own).

The 9th Queen's Royal Lancers and the 12th Royal Lancers (Prince of Wales's) were amalgamated in September 1960 under the new name of 9th/12th Royal Lancers (Prince of Wales's).

The 4th/7th Royal Dragoon Guards and the 17th/21st Lancers are the only two regiments still wearing their old wartime badges, although now made in anodised metal. Some others changed to the St Edward's Crown and the Prussian Eagle of the 14th/20th King's Hussars at present is black, with gilded orb and sceptre.

Plate 3. Cap Badges
Arms and Services

Shortly after World War 2 a number of corps were granted the title 'Royal' in recognition of service rendered during the War: they were the Corps of Royal Military Police, The Royal Army Educational Corps, the Royal

Army Dental Corps and the Royal Pioneer Corps. The R.A.E.C. and the R.A.D.C. changed cap badges as well; the former adopted the symbolic torch of learning and the latter a dragon's head holding a sword with its teeth. New cap badges were also made for the M.P.s, with the title 'Royal' added in the scroll.

The cap badge of the Corps of Royal Engineers, then still with the 'GRVI' cypher and King's crown, was slightly changed after the war as new issues were made with a white metal wreath.

The scroll of the Royal Army Medical Corps's cap badge was changed to white metal, the motto *In Arduis Fidelis* replacing the Corps title.

After the War new cap badges were also issued to the Royal Corps of Signals, the Royal Army Ordnance Corps and the Royal Electrical and Mechanical Engineers.

During the reigns of George VI and Elizabeth II the cap badges of the Royal Army Service Corps's officers were made of silver (or chromed white metal), gilt and enamel, and those of other ranks were made of brass.

On 15 July 1965 the R.A.S.C. became the Royal Corps of Transport and, although the basic design of the badges was not altered, the new title was inscribed on the scroll and new anodised bi-metal badges were issued to the other ranks.

The Army Air Corps was formed in 1942 and its badges were worn by the Parachute Regiment and by the Glider Pilot Regiment. The year after a new badge was issued for the Parachute Regiment while the Glider Pilot Regiment continued to wear A.A.C. badges until 1950, when the A.A.C. was disbanded and a proper badge was adopted for the Glider Pilot Regiment. In due time, in 1957, the G.P.R. was also disbanded and its personnel taken over by the newly-raised Army Air Corps.

A new badge was adopted by the Army Air Corps in 1957, somewhat similar to the 1942 pattern, but without the lettering 'A.A.C.' Beret badges are worn on a dark blue square backing, and personnel of R.A.M.C., R.A.P.C., etc, attached to the A.A.C., wear their own cap badges on the blue backing.

After 1953, with the accession to the throne of Elizabeth II, all the crowns and cyphers were changed to those of the new monarch. The cap badge of the Military Provost Staff Corps is a good example as the crowned cypher is actually its badge. New badges were issued also to the Royal Horse Artillery, with the new crown and cypher, while only the crown was changed in the case of the Royal Artillery, Royal Armoured Corps, Royal Tank Regiment and Royal Army Veterinary Corps.

Plate 4. Cap Badges
Arms and Services

The crown was also changed on the badges of the Royal Army Pay Corps, Royal Pioneer Corps, Intelligence Corps, etc., illustrated in this plate. The General Service Corps has now only one badge and it also has a different role, while the former badge of the G.S.C. (Training Units) is now worn by the Junior Leaders Training Regiment.

A small white metal brazier was added to the all-brass cap badges of the Army Catering Corps after the War and, in 1973, a scroll with the words 'We Sustain' was added at the bottom.

The Mobile Defence Corps was created in 1955 as a link between the Armed Forces and the Civil Defence Forces; it was disbanded in 1959. The Special Air Service was raised in 1940 and ten years later became part of the Regular Army as a regiment.

The Women's Royal Army Corps and Queen Alexandra's Royal Army Nursing Corps were both formed on 1 February 1949 as part of the Regular Army. They are the successors of previous women's services which were raised during both World Wars.

The badge of the Army Legal Services was adopted in 1958; the officers previously appointed to the Army Legal Services Staff wore the Royal Crest, the badge of the Extra-Regimentally Employed List.

The wording on the badge of the Army Department Fire Service has been slightly changed as the letters 'W.D.' (War Department) have since disappeared and the title now reads 'Army Fire Service'.

The badge of the Royal Hospital, Chelsea, was adopted in 1945 and it is worn by the Hospital's staff.

Plate 5. Cap Badges
Miscellanea

The Control Commission, Germany, was a post-war organisation formed in the British Zone of occupied Germany. Its personnel also wore a special formation sign, illustrated on Plate 14.

The War Department Constabulary and the War Department Police (Cyprus) changed their titles in 1964: the former became the Army Department Constabulary and the latter the Army Department Police (Cyprus) and is now a depot.

The Royal Military School of Music is at Kneller Hall, Twickenham, Middlesex, and its badge was adopted in 1907. The Small Arms School Corps was formed in 1929 by the previous (1926) amalgamation of the Small Arms School and Machine Gun School. The Royal Military Academy and the Mons Officer Cadet School both train the future officers of the British Army.

Foot Guards

The cap badges of the five regiments of the Foot Guards have remained the same, with the exception of that worn by warrant officers, N.C.O.s and musicians of the Grenadier Guards, whose cypher has been changed to that of the reigning monarch. All guardsmen now wear badges made of anodised metal.

Plate 6. Cap Badges
The Brigade of Gurkhas

Gurkha soldiers have fought for the British Crown since the Pindaree War of 1817 and in 1825, at Bhurtpore, they gained their first battle honour. In 1947 there were ten Gurkha regiments and on 1 January 1948 four of these became part of the British Army while the others remained in the new Indian Army. The four regiments, together with the Gurkha Engineers, Signals, Transport Regiment, the 5th Gurkha Dog Company and the Gurkha Independent Parachute Company, were formed into the Brigade of Gurkhas which later became the bulk of the 17th Division, formed by the 48th, 63rd and 99th Gurkha Infantry Brigades (Plate 13) and other British units.

After peace was re-established in Borneo the Gurkhas were regrouped once again into the Brigade of Gurkhas, but now at reduced strength.

The 2nd King Edward VII's Own Gurkha Rifles (The Sirmoor Rifles) was raised in 1815 as the Sirmoor Battalion. The 6th Queen Elizabeth's Own Gurkha Rifles was raised in 1817, and designated the 6th Gurkha Rifles in 1903, and it assumed the present title on 1 January 1959. On the same date, the 7th Gurkha Rifles, originally raised in 1902, became the 7th Duke of Edinburgh's Own Gurkha Rifles. The 10th Princess Mary's Own Gurkha Rifles was raised in 1890 as the 1st Regiment of Burma Infantry; it became the 10th Gurkha Rifles in 1901 and Princess Mary's Regiment in 1949.

The officers wear a regimental badge similar to that of the other ranks on the slouch hat while on the peaked cap, forage cap and beret they wear a small replica of the same badge on a coloured cord boss; red for the 2nd and black for the other regiments and for the Engineers. The officers of the Sirmoor Rifles have a red and green diced cloth backing under the slouch hat badge, the other ranks wear black badges on red backing. The small badge worn on the cord boss by the officers of the 10th Gurkha Rifles has no scroll.

The Royal Crown and the cypher of the Duke of Edinburgh were added on the badges of the 6th and 7th Gurkha Rifles in 1959 when they became affiliated to the Queen and the Duke of Edinburgh.

The Gurkha Engineers, Signals, Transport Regiment and Military

Police were all formed after 1948 and the last was disbanded in 1965. The Transport Regiment was formed in 1958 as the Gurkha Army Service Corps: it was renamed the Gurkha Transport Regiment in 1965.

A cap badge similar to that of the Staff Band, but with 'Boys' between the handles of the kukris, is worn by the Boys' Company.

Infantry Regiments

In 1946 the title 'Royal' was granted to the Lincolnshire, Leicestershire, and Hampshire Regiments in recognition of their past service, and the new title was added onto their cap badges. In the case of the Royal Lincolnshire, the word 'Egypt', on a tablet below the Sphinx, was changed from Old English to modern lettering.

In 1951 the Dorsetshire Regiment was renamed the Dorset Regiment and its title changed on the scroll. The following year a new badge was granted to the Green Howards (Alexandra, Princess of Wales's Own Yorkshire Regiment). It should be mentioned that there are two versions of the previous cap badge of the Green Howards as, during World War 2, some were made with the king's crown instead of the traditional coronet.

In 1956 Prince Alfred's cypher in the centre of the Wiltshire Regiment's cap badge was changed to that of Philip, Duke of Edinburgh, who in 1954 became Colonel-in-Chief of the regiment.

Two years later the Rifle Brigade adopted a new cap badge, with a Guelphic crown and without battle honours on the surrounding wreath. Sometime after World War 2 the fleur-de-lis of the Manchester Regiment and the cap badge of the King's Own Yorkshire Light Infantry were changed to white metal.

Post-War Reorganisation of the British Army (Brigades)

Traditionally, each regiment of the British infantry was composed of two regular battalions and a number of territorial battalions. One regular battalion was normally at home and the other overseas so that a man's service could be spent partly in Britain and partly abroad, still in the same regiment. After World War 2 the Army was reorganised and the infantry regiments lost their second regular battalion.

In 1947 all the battalions were organised into the Training Brigade Groups (Plate 12), each battalion representing its regiment.

Following the recommendations contained in the 1957 White Paper all the regiments of the Infantry of the Line were grouped into fourteen brigades, as far as possible on the basis of regional affinity. Each brigade should have been composed of three or four battalions, each representing a regiment of the 1957 Regular Army. However, as there were too many battalions to fit into the fourteen brigades, a number of regimental amalgamations became necessary.

Between the years 1958 and 1961 the following amalgamations took place:

20 January 1959
The Royal Scots Fusiliers   ⎫ The Royal Highland Fusiliers
The Highland Light Infantry   ⎬ (Princess Margaret's Own Glasgow
  (City of Glasgow Regiment)   ⎭   and Ayrshire Regiment)

14 October 1959
The Queen's Royal Regiment (West Surrey) ⎱ The Queen's Royal Surrey
The East Surrey Regiment   ⎰   Regiment

1 March 1961
The Buffs (Royal East Kent Regiment)   ⎱ The Queen's Own Buffs,
The Queen's Own Royal West Kent Regiment ⎰   The Royal Kent Regiment

1 October 1959
The King's Own Royal Regiment (Lancaster) ⎱ The King's Own Royal
The Border Regiment   ⎰   Border Regiment

1 September 1958
The King's Regiment (Liverpool) ⎱ The King's Regiment (Manchester and
The Manchester Regiment   ⎰   Liverpool)

1 July 1958
The East Lancashire Regiment   ⎫ The Lancashire Regiment
The South Lancashire Regiment   ⎬   (Prince of Wales's Volunteers)
  (The Prince of Wales's Volunteers) ⎭

29 August 1959
The Royal Norfolk Regiment ⎱ 1st East Anglian Regiment (Royal Norfolk
The Suffolk Regiment   ⎰   and Suffolk

1 June 1960
The Royal Lincolnshire Regiment ⎫ 2nd East Anglian Regiment (Duchess of
The Northamptonshire Regiment   ⎬   Gloucester's Own Royal Lincolnshire
                                ⎭   and Northamptonshire)

2 June 1958
The Bedfordshire and Hertfordshire Regiment ⎱ 3rd East Anglian Regiment
The Essex Regiment   ⎰   (16th/44th)

17 May 1958
The Devonshire Regiment ⎱ The Devonshire and Dorset Regiment
The Dorset Regiment   ⎰

9 June 1959

The Royal Berkshire Regiment
(Princess Charlotte of Wales's)
The Wiltshire Regiment (Duke of Edinburgh's) } The Duke of Edinburgh's Royal Regiment (Berkshire and Wiltshire)

6 October 1959

The Somerset Light Infantry (Prince Albert's)
The Duke of Cornwall's Light Infantry } The Somerset and Cornwall Light Infantry

25 April 1958

The West Yorkshire Regiment
(The Prince of Wales's Own)
The East Yorkshire Regiment
(The Duke of York's Own) } The Prince of Wales's Own Regiment of Yorkshire

31 January 1959

The South Staffordshire Regiment
The North Staffordshire Regiment
(The Prince of Wales's) } The Staffordshire Regiment (The Prince of Wales's)

7 February 1961

The Seaforth Highlanders (Ross-shire Buffs, The Duke of Albany's)
The Queen's Own Cameron Highlanders } The Queen's Own Highlanders (Seaforth and Camerons)

Plate 7. Cap Badges
Brigades

The remaining infantry regiments, reduced to battalion strength, were grouped into fourteen brigades whose personnel wore brigade cap badges and regimental collar badges. The Midland Brigade was retitled Forester Brigade and was disbanded in 1963.

The following is the list of these brigades with their component regiments:

The Lowland Brigade
  The Royal Scots (The Royal Regiment)
  The Royal Highland Fusiliers (Princess Margaret's Own Glasgow and Ayrshire Regiment)
  The King's Own Scottish Borderers
  The Cameronians (Scottish Rifles)

The Home Counties Brigade
  The Queen's Royal Surrey Regiment
  The Queen's Own Buffs, The Royal Kent Regiment
  The Royal Sussex Regiment
  The Middlesex Regiment (Duke of Cambridge's Own)

The Lancastrian Brigade
    The King's Own Royal Border Regiment
    The King's Regiment (Manchester and Liverpool)
    The Lancashire Regiment (Prince of Wales's Volunteers)
    The Loyal Regiment (North Lancashire)

The Fusilier Brigade
    The Royal Northumberland Fusiliers
    The Royal Fusiliers (City of London Regiment)
    The Lancashire Fusiliers
    The Royal Warwickshire Fusiliers — formerly part of the Forester Brigade

The Midland Brigade — retitled Forester Brigade — disbanded in 1963
    The Royal Warwickshire Regiment
    The Royal Leicestershire Regiment
    The Sherwood Foresters (Nottinghamshire and Derbyshire Regiment)

The East Anglian Brigade
    1st East Anglian Regiment (Royal Norfolk and Suffolk)
    2nd East Anglian Regiment (Duchess of Gloucester's Own Royal Lincolnshire
        and Northamptonshire)
    3rd East Anglian Regiment (16th/44th)
    The Royal Leicestershire Regiment — formerly part of the Forester Brigade

The Wessex Brigade
    The Devonshire and Dorset Regiment
    The Gloucestershire Regiment
    The Royal Hampshire Regiment
    The Duke of Edinburgh's Royal Regiment (Berkshire and Wiltshire)

The Light Infantry Brigade
    The Somerset and Cornwall Light Infantry
    The King's Own Yorkshire Light Infantry
    The King's Shropshire Light Infantry
    The Durham Light Infantry

The Yorkshire Brigade
    The Prince of Wales's Own Regiment of Yorkshire
    The Green Howards (Alexandra, Princess of Wales's Own Yorkshire Regiment)
    The Duke of Wellington's Regiment (West Riding)
    The York and Lancaster Regiment

The Mercian Brigade
    The Cheshire Regiment
    The Worcestershire Regiment
    The Staffordshire Regiment (The Prince of Wales's)
    The Sherwood Foresters (Nottinghamshire and Derbyshire Regiment) —
        formerly part of the Forester Brigade

The Welsh Brigade
 The Royal Welch Fusiliers
 The South Wales Borderers
 The Welch Regiment

The North Irish Brigade
 The Royal Inniskilling Fusiliers
 The Royal Ulster Rifles
 The Royal Irish Fusiliers

The Highland Brigade
 The Black Watch (Royal Highland Regiment)
 Queen's Own Highlanders (Seaforth and Camerons)
 The Gordon Highlanders
 The Argyll and Sutherland Highlanders (Princess Louise's)

The Green Jackets Brigade
 1st Green Jackets (43rd/52nd)
 2nd Green Jackets (The King's Royal Rifle Corps)
 3rd Green Jackets (The Rifle Brigade)

Officers' and other ranks' versions of the brigade cap badges have been used during the decade of their existence. The former wore gilded and silver plated badges as a rule, the latter anodised badges, although some embroidered and enamelled variations have been made for the officers. There are also two sizes of the officer's cap badge of the East Anglian Brigade.

Some regiments used to wear coloured cloth backings under the cap badges, for instance the Lancashire Regiment wore a $1\frac{1}{4}$-in. square yellow backing, the King's Own Royal Border Regiment a $1\frac{3}{4}$-in. square scarlet backing, and the King's Regiment a $1\frac{3}{4} \times 2$-in. scarlet backing. All three were part of the Lancastrian Brigade.

Divisions

The brigades lasted until 1968 when, on 1 July, the infantry was reorganised into the divisional structure. Six divisions were created, each formed by a number of regiments; thus the brigade cap badges were gradually replaced by regimental cap badges.

The Brigade of Guards became the Guards Division, formed by the old five regiments: the Grenadier, Coldstream, Scots, Irish and Welsh Guards.

A list of the other divisions, with their component regiments, is given below:

The Queen's Division
    The Queen's Regiment
    The Royal Regiment of Fusiliers
    The Royal Anglian Regiment

The King's Division
    The King's Own Royal Border Regiment
    The King's Regiment (Manchester and Liverpool)
    The Prince of Wales's Own Regiment of Yorkshire
    The Green Howards (Alexandra, Princess of Wales's Own Yorkshire Regiment)
    The Royal Irish Rangers (27th (Inniskilling) 83rd and 87th)
    The Queen's Lancashire Regiment
    The Duke of Wellington's Regiment (West Riding)

The Prince of Wales's Division
    The Devonshire and Dorset Regiment
    The Cheshire Regiment
    The Royal Welch Fusiliers
    The Royal Regiment of Wales (24th/41st Foot)
    The Gloucestershire Regiment
    The Worcestershire and Sherwood Foresters Regiment (29th/45th Foot)
    The Royal Hampshire Regiment
    The Staffordshire Regiment (The Prince of Wales's)
    The Duke of Edinburgh's Royal Regiment (Berkshire and Wiltshire)

The Scottish Division
    The Royal Scots (The Royal Regiment)
    The Royal Highland Fusiliers (Princess Margaret's Own Glasgow and Ayrshire
        Regiment)
    The King's Own Scottish Borderers
    The Black Watch (Royal Highland Regiment)
    Queen's Own Highlanders (Seaforth and Camerons)
    The Gordon Highlanders
    The Argyll and Sutherland Highlanders (Princess Louise's)

The Light Division
    The Light Infantry
    The Royal Green Jackets

Plate 8. Cap Badges
Infantry Regiments

The Home Counties Brigade was reorganised as a 'large' regiment on 31 December 1966. The newly-born Queen's Regiment was formed by four battalions:

    1st Bn The Queen's Regiment (Queen's Surreys)
    2nd Bn The Queen's Regiment (Queen's Own Buffs)

3rd Bn The Queen's Regiment (Royal Sussex)
4th Bn The Queen's Regiment (Middlesex)

A new cap badge and new collar badge were adopted, incorporating the motifs of the four previous regimental badges.

On 23 April 1968 (St George's Day) the Fusiliers Brigade became the Royal Regiment of Fusiliers, composed of the former Brigade's four battalions.

The Brigade's cap badge and collar badges were retained by the Regiment, but the red and white hackle was adopted by all the battalions, instead of the different colours previously worn.

The third regiment of the Queen's Division is the Royal Anglian Regiment, which was formed on 1 September 1964 from the East Anglian Brigade. Its battalions are:

1st (Norfolk and Suffolk) Bn
2nd (Duchess of Gloucester's Own Lincolnshire and Northamps) Bn
3rd (16th/44th Foot) Bn
4th (Leicestershire) Bn, the Royal Anglian Regiment

The design of the cap badge remained similar to that of the Brigade; however the title in the scroll was changed to 'Royal Anglian'. Each battalion retained its individual collar badge.

The King's Division was formed on 1 July 1968 by the Lancastrian and Yorkshire Brigade and by the Royal Irish Rangers, formerly the North Irish Brigade.

The Lancastrian Brigade contributed three regiments only, as the Lancashire Regiment (Prince of Wales's Volunteers) and the Loyal Regiment (North Lancashire) were amalgamated in March 1970 to form the Queen's Lancashire Regiment. New cap badges were issued to all three regiments.

The York and Lancaster Regiment, of the Yorkshire Brigade, was disbanded in December 1968 and the remaining three regiments joined the King's Division. The Duke of Wellington's Regiment (West Riding) resumed its old pre-1958 cap badge, while the other two regiments adopted new ones.

On 1 July 1968 the North Irish Brigade was converted into one regiment, the Royal Irish Rangers, formed by three battalions. The 3rd Battalion was disbanded at Catterick in December 1968, and its operational role was taken over by the 1st Battalion, which moved up to Catterick from Worcester. The battalions are known simply as the 1st and 2nd Bns of the Royal Irish Rangers. The regimental cap badge is similar to that of the Brigade except for the title scroll which now reads 'Royal Irish Rangers'. A new collar badge has also been adopted.

The Wessex, Mercian and Welsh Brigades contributed to the formation of the Prince of Wales's Division.

The four battalions of the Wessex Brigade regained regimental status, although the Glosters and the Royal Hampshires were due to amalgamate in 1970. The latter readopted their old regimental cap badges while the other two regiments, the Devonshire and Dorset and the Duke of Edinburgh's, used their previous brigade's collar badges as head-dress badges.

The Worcestershire Regiment and the Sherwood Foresters were amalgamated at Bulford on 28 February 1970 and a 'combined' cap badge was adopted by the new regiment known as the Worcestershire & Sherwood Foresters. The other two units of the Mercian Brigade, the Cheshire and the Staffordshire Regiments, became independent regiments, the former with its old cap badge while the latter adopted its previous collar badge as cap badge.

The Welsh Brigade contributed with only two regiments as, in 1969, the South Wales Borderers and the Welch Regiment were merged to form the Royal Regiment of Wales (24th/41st Foot).

The Royal Welch Fusiliers resumed their own pre-1958 regimental cap badge.

The Scottish Division was formed on 1 July 1968 by the Lowland and Highland Brigades. Originally, it was planned to disband the fourth regiment of each brigade, but only the Cameronians (Scottish Rifles) were disbanded in May 1968; the Argyll and Sutherland Highlanders were reduced to a small 'tradition' detachment, the Balaklava Company. One year after, however, the Argylls were back, at battalion strength, as a regiment of the Scottish Division.

New cap badges were adopted by the Royal Highland Fusiliers (Princess Margaret's Own Glasgow and Ayrshire Regiment) and Queen's Own Highlanders (Seaforth and Camerons) while the other regiments were issued with pre-1958 badges, now made of anodised metal.

The Light Division was formed by two newly-constituted regiments: the Light Infantry and the Royal Green Jackets.

The Light Infantry Brigade became a regiment on 10 July 1968 (Light Infantry Day) and the Brigade's four regiments became the 1st, 2nd, 3rd and 4th Bns, The Light Infantry. The cap badge remained that of the Light Infantry Brigade and a smaller version of it was adopted as a regimental collar badge. As is usual for bugle badges, they are worn in pairs, mouthpieces towards the opening of the collar.

Already in 1958 the battalions of the Green Jackets Brigade had established a common drill, except for the mess kit and the regimental titles worn on the shoulder straps. Although remaining regiments in theory, the components of the Brigade assumed numerical Battalion denomination and finally, on 1 January 1966, the Brigade was redesignated the Royal Green Jackets, a 'large' regiment composed of the following battalions:

1st Bn the Royal Green Jackets (43rd & 52nd)
2nd Bn The Royal Green Jackets (The King's Royal Rifle Corps)
3rd Bn The Royal Green Jackets (The Rifle Brigade)

A new cap badge was adopted by the regiment and on 15 June 1968 a new shoulder title, the same for all three battalions, was taken into use. It consists of the letters 'RGJ' in Old English script, surmounted by a bugle.

The process of amalgamation and integration of these regiments has been long and painful. Several of them, already reduced to company strength, were subsequently reformed as battalions. The projected amalgamation of the Gloucestershire and Royal Hampshire Regiments should have taken place in 1970. A new cap badge was made for the new regiment which, however, never materialised.

Plate 9. Other Cap Badges

Field-Marshals wear an embroidered cap badge consisting of two crossed batons on a wreath, surmounted by the Royal Crest. Generals wear a similar badge but with a sword and a baton, instead of crossed batons, in its centre. Brigadiers and Substantive (full) Colonels wear only the Royal Crest.

Field-Marshals and Generals (including Chaplains-General) are also entitled to a double row of gold oak leaves on the visor of the peaked cap and the Brigadiers and Substantive Colonels (including chaplains of equivalent rank), to one row only, embroidered at the front of the visor.

Field officers (not Rifle and Light Infantry regiments) have a plain gold $\frac{3}{4}$-in. stripe, while field officers of the Rifle regiments wear one row of black oak leaves and those of the Light Infantry regiments a silver $\frac{3}{4}$-in. stripe.

The officers below field rank wear peaked caps with plain visor, although gold stripes are worn by all officers of some regiments and gold or brass stripes by the other ranks of the Guards.

The chaplains, both Christian and Jewish, are all officers and wear cap badges made of silver, gilt and enamel, or plain black ones.

A special badge is worn by personnel of the Army Department Fleet, formerly known as the War Department Fleet. The formation sign worn by these units is shown on Plate 16.

Formation Signs

A great number of wartime formation signs which were worn on the upper sleeve were kept in use for years after World War 2 and many are still worn nowadays. Due to the post-war reorganisation of the British Army many new formation signs have been adopted as well. However, the great majority of World War 2 signs have by now (1973) disappeared and the old ones still in use are normally slightly different from the originals; thus they can easily be recognised as modern patterns.

As it is difficult to separate the signs of the Regular Army from those worn by the territorials without creating confusion, both types have been illustrated together. Many of these had already been adopted during the last war but were in use after the War as well.

Formation signs worn by units smaller than brigades have not been included.

Plate 10. Formation Signs
Home Commands

During World War 2 the United Kingdom was militarily divided into Home Commands which, in turn, were divided into Districts. The same organisation, although modified in its structure, was maintained for many years after the War.

The South-Eastern Command was disbanded in 1944 and its former territory absorbed by the Southern and Eastern Commands. The formation sign of the latter was changed in 1947 and also, during the same year, the small sign of the Northern Command was replaced by the shield-shaped badge.

The Northumbrian District, the North Midland District and the three Yorkshire Ridings were all part of the Northern Command.

The badge of the Southern Command is based on a simplified design of the Southern Cross constellation and each branch of service of the Command wore the same badge, but in its arm-of-service colours. Miscellaneous units of the Southern Command wore their own sign, horizontally divided into black and red; however, some embroidered signs have been made with dark blue, instead of black, felt at the top. The colours have also been misplaced on some other Southern Command formation signs as in the case of the last shield illustrated, worn by the R.A.D.C. Note the difference between this badge and the one above, which is the correct one.

Garrisons and Other Formations

The formation sign of the Orkney and Shetland Defences was a red fouled anchor embroidered on dark blue felt. The same anchor, but smaller and on a round background, was adopted after the War by the local T.A. units, nominally the Orkney and Zetland Battery, 540 Regt (The Lovat Scouts), R.A.

After the War the White Rose of Yorkshire on a black background became the emblem of the East and West Ridings Area (Northern Command) and the Tudor Rose was adopted by the newly-formed Catterick

District in 1947. The District previously had been part of the Northumbrian and also of the North Riding Districts and, in 1952, it became part of the Northumbrian District once again. In the 1960s Catterick Camp was the headquarters of the Yorkshire District and the Tudor Rose on green background was the formation sign of the District. Northumbrian District ceased to exist on 31 December 1972 and the new North East District with headquarters in York took over all the territories previously controlled by Northumbrian and Yorkshire Districts.

The formation sign of Force 135 (Channel Islands Liberation Force) represents the three lions of the arms of Jersey and Guernsey.

There are two patterns of the Anti-Aircraft Command's formation sign, both in embroidered and printed variations. The main difference is that in the first pattern the bow was round, and without the handle.

The British troops in Northern Ireland and the personnel of 6th Corps wore a similar sign, the former a red gate and the latter a green gate, both on black rectangular background.

Plate 11. Formation Signs
Districts

All the Scottish districts belonged to the Scottish Command; only two districts remained after the War, the Highland District, now wearing the formation sign of the former North Highland District, and the Lowland District, with the sign of the former West Scotland District.

The first formation sign of the Northern Ireland District showed a bird in a nest (the Latin for nest is *nid*). Subsequently, the badge was changed to the typical 'Irish' gate, in white on emerald green background.

The formation sign of the West Lancashire District consists of the emblems of Cheshire, Lancashire and Staffordshire. It ceased to exist in 1944 when its territory was absorbed by its neighbouring districts of Western Command: the Lancashire and Border District, renamed North Western District, and the North Wales District, which became the Midland West District.

The Central Midland District was renamed East Central District and remained part of the Eastern Command.

The County of Essex was initially administered by the 2nd Corps and, subsequently, by the Essex and Suffolk District (Eastern Command) whose formation sign depicted the Suffolk Castle and the Seaxes of Essex on a shield, in full colour. The colours were changed to black and yellow in 1944 when it became part of the East Anglian District and, finally, in 1946 the District adopted the viking's head as its emblem.

The disbandment of the South-Eastern Command in 1944 also caused many changes in the organisation of the Southern District: the Hampshire and Dorset District became the Aldershot and Hampshire District and

Dorset joined Wiltshire (previously Salisbury Plain District) to form the new Wiltshire and Dorset District. Most of the forces which invaded Europe in June 1944 embarked from the counties of Hampshire and Dorset; thus the District's badge symbolises Victory setting out for the invasion. The Aldershot District was formed in 1948.

During the war the North Kent and Surrey District (South-Eastern Command) used two formation signs both depicting the rampant White Horse of Kent. The first badge was round and showed only the horse's head.

A Canadian Corps administered the area that later became the Sussex District of South-Eastern Command. The East Kent District, also, was part of the same Command and later, as Home Counties District, it became part of the Eastern Command.

The reorganisation of several districts has taken place since the war and many badges have been abolished or modified. The St Oswald's Shield in the formation sign of the Northumbrian District, initially composed of six red and yellow stripes, was later changed to eight stripes and the francolin partridge of the South Western District (Southern Command) was replaced by the Golden Hind on a green background. The London District was part of the Southern Command.

The bell in the formation sign of the South Midland District (Southern Command) is the Great Tom of Christ Church, Oxford, and the archer in the badge of the North Midland District (Northern Command) is Robin Hood. In 1948 a new formation sign depicting the Irish Harp was adopted by the North Ireland District.

Plate 12. Formation Signs
Army Corps

The 1st Corps was reformed in Germany in the early 1950s and, once again, the white spearhead became its emblem. It should be noted that during the War each branch of service of the Corps wore the spearhead on a background divided in arm-of-service colours.

The first pattern of the 2nd Corps badge was a fish on a blue and white wavy background but later a much simpler badge was devised, similar to that of 1st Corps. It is a figure '2' on a red diamond.

Divisions

The white triangle of the 1st Infantry Division symbolically stands for the top of the spearhead of the 1st Corps badge, as the Division is the first division of 1st Corps. This formation sign used to be on a black or khaki background or on its own. Specimens can also be found with a narrow red edging, worn by infantry units, or with yellow edging for the divisional armoured units. The divisional artillery, signals, etc., wear the white triangle on a diamond-shaped background of arm-of-service colours.

The formation sign of the 4th Division initially was the fourth quadrant of a circle made of red felt. Later it was changed to a red circle with the fourth quadrant detached, on a white background. A third pattern has since been adopted in printed or woven variations, similar to the second but on a black background.

The 40th Division was formed in 1949 and took part in the Korean War. Its badge is represented by a cockerel on a black square or rectangular background and originates from a similar badge worn by the homonymous division during World War 1.

The 1st Commonwealth Division also fought in Korea and was raised out there from British and Commonwealth troops in 1951. There are in existence two slightly different variations of the same badge.

The 42nd (Lancashire) Division was raised in 1947 as one of the new territorial divisions, in place of the 42nd (East Lancashire) and 55th (West Lancashire). The new divisional sign incorporates the red diamond of the 42nd and the red rose of the 55th Divisions.

The wartime badge of the 44th (Home Counties) Division was a plain red oval which in 1947 was combined with the shield of the East Kent District, and later changed to a third pattern, with a yellow trident in its centre.

Both 48th (South Midlands) and 54th (East Anglian) Divisions adopted brand new formation signs when they were re-raised after the war as T.A. divisions. The Saxon Crown is the centrepiece of both badges.

In 1947 the 56th (London) Division became an armoured T.A. division and adopted a new emblem, the knight's helmet and the sword, more suited to its new role. In 1950, however, the wartime badge, Dick Whittington's Cat, was resumed, now with a sword superimposed on the cat.

Another black cat, but on a khaki background, was the badge of the 17th Indian Division from 1943. Later the background was changed to yellow and the Division became the 17th British Division in Malaya, which in 1965 became the Malaya District.

The badge of the 17th Gurkha Division was worn during the War by the 43rd Lorried Infantry Brigade.

Some other divisions have been reformed as well in the last twenty-eight years but wear their old wartime formation signs. Some brigades wear old divisional signs. Although the design of these badges has remained the same, the manufacture has often changed. There are now formation signs of the 6th Armoured Division with the mailed fist on a blue background and many modern badges are considerably smaller than their wartime counterparts.

Training Brigade Groups

The first post-war army reorganisation took place in 1947 with the creation of the Training Brigade Groups, intended to group the existing infantry regiments on the basis of their regional affinity.

Each group wore a new formation sign, embroidered on felt or printed, on the left sleeve of the battledress.

Plate 13. Formation Signs
Brigades

A number of these formation signs used to be worn during the War and others have been adopted since 1945.

The 1st and 4th Guards Brigades have readopted the old badge of the Guards Armoured Division with the addition of Roman figures 'I' and 'IV' below the eye. The 2nd Guards Brigade's badge was adopted in Malaya in 1947 whilst the 2nd Infantry Brigade initially wore the white triangle of the 1st Division, later changed to the badge illustrated.

The 3rd was an Infantry Brigade Group. After the War the 2nd Division was stationed in the Far East and its 5th Brigade was part of the British Commonwealth Occupational Forces in Japan. In 1946 the 53rd (Welsh) Division, then in Europe, was renamed the 2nd Division. Thus the 4th, 5th and 6th Brigades of the latter, still in the Far East, became independent and were renumbered the 24th, 25th and 26th Independent Infantry Brigades. The 5th Brigade had the same sign as the 2nd Division, but slightly smaller and, as 25th Independent Infantry Brigade, adopted a new formation sign which incorporated the divisional crossed keys and a 'Torii' gate to commemorate its service in Japan. Only one key, crossed with a bayonet, is shown in the latest badge of the 5th Infantry Brigade and the 6th has the same motif but with inverted colours. The 8th is also an Infantry Brigade and the 11th used to wear the woven formation sign of the former 78th Division. There are two versions of the 12th Infantry Brigade badge as the H.Q. personnel wore a fouled anchor on a blue diamond. The personnel of the 17th Infantry Brigade also wore two different badges; the triangular one symbolised the Nile Delta but later, in 1952, it was changed to a yellow arrow pointing upwards on a scarlet rectangle. The 18th Infantry Brigade was also composed of British and Gurkha units, thus a bayonet and a kukri are represented on its badge. The first pattern of the formation sign of the 19th Infantry Brigade had the top point of the triangle cut off; the second pattern is illustrated.

A penguin was the symbol of the 22nd Beach Brigade and the badge of the 264th (Scottish) Beach Brigade (T.A.) was composed of the St Andrew's Cross of the former 52nd (Lowland) Division and the sign of the Beach Groups (Plate 16). The 23rd, the 29th and the 72nd were the British

Brigade Groups stationed in India after the War. As well as the 25th Infantry Brigade there was a 25th Armoured Brigade which had a badge similar to that of the former 1st Armoured Division.

The badge of the 27th Independent Infantry Brigade was used until 1949, when the Brigade became part of the 40th Division; some have red and others yellow numerals.

The Cross of St Andrew is present in the formation sign of the 30th (Lowland) Independent Armoured Brigade (T.A.) and again in that of the 155th Independent Infantry Brigade.

Another three badges have been worn by T.A. units, namely the 107th (Ulster) Independent Brigade Group and the 161st and 162nd Independent Infantry Brigade Groups.

The 39th was also an Independent Infantry Brigade Group which has worn, in turn, two different badges. The 31st, 49th, 50th and 51st are Independent Infantry Brigades; the 160th and 302nd are Infantry Brigades.

The formation signs of the Brigades of Gurkhas are similar: they all show the crossed kukris on different coloured backgrounds.

Plate 14. Formation Signs
British Forces Overseas

A great number of formation signs have been worn by British forces stationed overseas but obvious space limitations compel me to show only part of these. Therefore I have purposely left out all the formation signs which, together with cap badges, I will be able to show, properly grouped into separate chapters, in another volume, i.e. Africa, India, West Indies, Gibraltar, Malta, etc.

Some of the badges illustrated have been worn during the War and others after the War. The designs of all the formation signs of the British Army of the Rhine (B.A.O.R.) derive from that of the 21st Army Group which became the B.A.O.R. in 1945. The blue cross on red or yellow shields was worn by line of communication troops in France and in the Netherlands respectively. The British troops in Berlin originally wore a red ring on a black circle and the title was added only in 1952.

In 1945 the 8th Army occupied Austria while its 13th Corps remained in the North-East of Italy where it became the British Element Trieste Force (BETFOR). In Austria the former 8th Army sign was usually worn and the personnel of the Allied Commission, Austria, wore the same badge with the letters 'ACA' added above the shield. Personnel of the H.Q. British Commonwealth Forces in Japan wore the formation sign which later was adopted by the British Commonwealth Forces in Korea.

The Cyrenaica and Tripolitania Districts were administrative organisations created during the war. The first pattern of the Cyrenaica District's badge was black on a white background and some slightly different variations exist of the Tripolitania District's badge as well. A Malayan kris on maroon background was the badge of the H.Q. Commonwealth Overseas Land Force.

The two small white triangles in the badge in the Canal South District (Middle East Land Forces) stand for a boat's sail and its reflection in Suez Canal waters. In the badge of the Canal North District the boat is at the top right of the formation sign. A blue fish was the emblem of the North Palestine District.

Plate 15. Formation Signs
Army Groups, Royal Artillery

Regular and Territorial Army formation signs of the A.G.R.A. have been illustrated side by side and the backgrounds of most show the colours of the Royal Artillery, red and blue.

The 2nd A.G.R.A. adopted the symbol of Taurus, the second sign of the zodiac, whilst the 86th A.G.R.A. (T.A.) wore the badge used by the 6th during the war, the sixth sign of the zodiac. The 3rd A.G.R.A. had two badges, a gun barrel and later the Roman 'III' on R.A. colours.

The 84th and 85th were Scottish territorial units and so was the 87th A.G.R.A. (Field), which used at one time to wear the badge of the 55th (West Lancashire) Division. The 88th, 89th, 90th and 91st were all Field Artillery units and most of the following were Anti-Aircraft Artillery units.

The formation sign of the 94th A.G.R.A. (A.A.) (T.A.) shows the Cheshire Garb and the Red Rose of Lancashire and that of the 96th, the Liver Buildings on the River Mersey. The Eros of Piccadilly Circus is the centrepiece of the formation sign of the 97th, a London A.A. unit.

An East Anglian windmill is depicted in the badge of the 98th and the Sussex Martlets is that of the 99th. The Hampshire Rose and the white and green bars of Wiltshire appear in the badge of the 100th A.G.R.A. (A.A.) (T.A.), together with the Royal Artillery colours.

Coast Brigades, Royal Artillery

Four Coast Brigades wore the three badges illustrated as the 102nd Brigade adopted the sign of the former 104th, a unit of Western Command. The 105th was a Scottish unit and all were part of the Territorial Army.

Anti-Aircraft Brigades, Royal Artillery

The 30th, 31st, 33rd and 34th Anti-Aircraft Brigades, R.A., wore their own formation signs; the 30th initially adopted a badge similar to that of the A.A. Command (Plate 10), later changed to the Roman 'XXX' on Royal Artillery colors.

A number of other Royal Artillery formation signs have been illustrated at the bottom of this plate: they mainly refer to training units. The Maritime Anti-Aircraft Artillery was formed in 1941 and consisted of A.A. gunners aboard ships which were not part of the Royal Navy. They wore a typical naval formation sign with the additional letters 'AA' which were later changed to 'R A' alongside the anchor.

Plate 16. Formation Signs
Engineer Groups
The Engineer Groups were all territorial units whose local connections were usually displayed on their formation signs. For instance, the first pattern of the sign of the 22nd Engineer Group (T.A.) was that of the Northumbrian District with the R.E. grenade embroidered on the St Oswald shield. The 24th Engineer Group (T.A.) had three different patterns of formation sign. The first one had a small replica of the badge of the 55th (West Lancashire) Division in its centre; in the second pattern the Staffordshire Knot was added below the rose and the final badge was a yellow shield with the Red Rose of Lancashire, the Cheshire Garb and the Staffordshire Knot. The 25th was a unit of Essex and the White Horse of Wiltshire was on the formation sign of the 26th. The 29th was a Scottish engineer group.

Port Task Forces, Royal Engineers
All three formation signs of the Port Task Forces have a blue background and depict marine symbols.

Some other formation signs illustrated in this plate belong to training units, depots and specialised branches of the Royal Engineers.

Miscellanea
The formation signs of the War Office and of the War Office Controlled Units were adopted in 1946; the Royal Crest of the latter now has the St Edward's Crown.

The Army, the Navy and the R.A.F. contributed in the formation of the Beach Groups, specialist units created for amphibious operations. They wore a special round badge with a red anchor within a red border, on a light blue background.

The War Department Fleet is known now as the Army Department Fleet and all its personnel wear a special formation sign and the cap badge illustrated on Plate 9. The service is composed of Royal Corps of Transport (former R.A.S.C.) personnel equipped with a variety of motor boats and amphibious crafts. The Air Despatch Group, R.A.S.C., was created in 1944 with the task of maintaining and supplying the ground forces by air. Its formation sign depicts a yellow Dakota aircraft on a rectangular blue background.

Formation signs of the Air Liaison Signals can also be found with the regimental numbers '2', '7' and '14' above the wings. The light blue, blue and green of the badge of the Air Formation Signals represent the sky, the sea and the land. The diving eagle is currently worn by all ranks of the Army Air Corps.

Poland

Poland became a unified nation in the tenth century and lost its independence in the eighteenth century and, more recently, in 1939 when it was invaded by the Germans and the Russians. After World War 2 Poland regained its national sovereignty on a territory which had moved considerably westwards.

The present Polish Army is descended from Polish units raised in the U.S.S.R. during World War 2. The first of these Polish formations was the 1st Tadeusz Kościuszko Infantry Division which was formed in 1943 and, as the new Polish Army advanced westwards, its ranks were swelled by Poles released from German concentration and prison camps. At the end of the War there were two Polish armies, the 1st and 2nd, whose ranks fought courageously at Lenino, Studzianki, and the Pommernstellung, to mention only a few names. Polish troops also took part in the capture of Berlin.

The first uniforms, adopted in 1943, were Russian ones on which Polish badges were worn accompanied by the characteristic square caps. However, as the months went by, their uniforms gradually assumed a more Polish appearance until, in 1945, except for minor details, they wore the same style uniforms as before the War.

The officers wore an ordinary and an evening uniform and all had square peaked caps, except for the officers of the Warsaw Infantry Division who wore rounded caps with a yellow band. The armoured troops used to wear khaki uniforms, as did the rest of the army, with orange cap bands and orange and black collar pennons, until 1947, when all ranks were issued with new steel-grey uniforms and rounded peaked caps. Their cap bands were initially steel-grey but, in 1949, black cap bands were introduced for all ranks. During these years the traditional square-topped peaked cap, known as the *czapka*, was gradually replaced by rounded caps until, during 1950–1, it was only permitted as head-dress for officers off duty.

The officers had winter and summer uniforms, technically divided into service and walking-out dress. The Sam Browne belt was usually worn without shoulder belt and the latter, together with pistol holder, was worn for field duties. The sword, decorations and medals were added for parade and ceremonial duties. The tunic with pointed collar and four patch pockets was the same as that used before the War. Tradition prescribed breeches for the cavalry, artillery and engineers and trousers for the rest of the army. The generals had two large blue stripes, divided

128

by blue piping, on the sides of the trousers and silver-embroidered zigzag ornaments on the cap band, collar patches and shoulder straps and on the cuffs of the tunic and greatcoat.

The other ranks were issued with summer and winter uniforms. The steel-grey uniforms of the armoured troops were replaced by khaki uniforms in 1950 and the generals' trouser stripes were changed from blue to light carmine and later, in 1958, they were changed back to blue.

In 1952 an evening dress, consisting of khaki peaked cap and tunic and dark blue trousers, was adopted for the officers. A new khaki jacket was adopted for service dress; it had an open collar showing the shirt and tie, and four patch pockets of Polish pattern, with rectangular flaps. A white tunic with buttoned-up collar and four patch pockets was also adopted.

In 1952, the colours of the cap bands, collar patches and piping were also reviewed; the generals had light carmine, the armoured and mechanised troops, black, and the rest of the army, dark carmine. However, the Warsaw Division kept the yellow cap bands and collar patches, now worn with dark carmine trouser stripes and piping. The internal security forces retained their old colours, i.e. the Internal Security Corps (*Korpus Bezpieczeństwa Wewnetrznego* – K.B.W.) wore dark blue and the Frontier Defence units (*Wojska Ochrony Pogranicza* – W.O.P.) wore light green. Later, in 1957, the newly-formed Army Security Units (*Wojskowa Służba Wewnętrzna* – W.S.W.) were given white cap bands and patches, and part of their equipment (belts, pistol holsters, etc.) was white as well. In the same year a maroon beret was adopted for all ranks of the newly-formed Airborne Division and in 1964 a light blue beret was adopted for the Coastal Defence units.

Armoured troops wore black berets. A brigade of mountain troops formed part of the Internal Security Corps: its personnel wore the traditional stiff feathered felt hat, the wide cape and dark blue patches with traditional zigzag on the collar of the tunic. The same uniform is still worn nowadays by these mountain troops, although jackets with an open collar have replaced the tunics, and collar patches are not used any more.

In 1952, when the jackets with open collar were adopted, new smaller patches were issued to fit the new collar. Metal badges were worn on these patches until, in 1960, the patches were abolished altogether and the year after a new set of collar badges was taken into use. In 1957 the coloured cap bands were abolished, except for those of the Warsaw Division, Internal Security Corps, Frontier Defence and Army Security units.

Double-breasted greatcoats were introduced in 1960 and at about that time new field uniforms were issued to all ranks. They are still in use at present although they have been modernised since introduction. The field uniforms are made of the typical olive-khaki striped material used by the armies of the Warsaw Pact.

Plate 17. Cap Badges

All ranks of the Polish Army wear the traditional Polish Eagle on all types of head-dress. The original eagle, worn until 1945 by the Polish armies in the West, used to be crowned, whilst the Polish armies in the East have worn the eagle without crown since 1944.

White metal cap badges (1) were worn by officers on the peaked cap until 1957 when peaked caps with brown visor and chin strap, and khaki cap bands, were introduced. In the following years the officers started to wear silver-embroidered badges (2) made in the shape of the previous metal cap badge. Another embroidered cap badge, slightly different (3), was adopted in 1970 for the regular officers while reserve officers continued wearing the old embroidered pattern.

The other ranks wear white metal oxidised badges on the peaked cap and machine-embroidered badges (4) on the field caps. These badges are embroidered in white thread on khaki, black, maroon and light blue felt; the backing felt matches the colours of the different head-dresses. There are two patterns of O.R.s' cap badges; as with the officers' badge, one was worn before and the other after 1970.

Since the War, two patterns of peaked cap have been used regardless of the shape of the crown (square or rounded). The cap worn until 1957 had black leather visor and chin strap; a metal rim around the visor was originally worn by the officers and later by all ranks. The generals had a silver zigzag embroidered all around the cap band, below a narrow stripe of braid; the senior officers wore a double stripe of braid at the top of the cap band and the junior officers had a single stripe. The rank of the wearer was shown by silver stars embroidered at the front, below the cap badge. Small silver chevrons and stripes, embroidered in place of the stars, showed N.C.O. rank.

The peaked cap of the 2nd pattern is in use at present. The rank stars, chevrons and stripes are still at the front, below the cap badge, but now the senior officers have two silver stripes on the brown leather visor, the junior officers one stripe only. Besides the two stripes on the visor, the generals have a silver zigzag embroidered on the cap band.

Plate 18. Officers' Rank Badges

The army rank badges are worn on the head-dress and, of course, on the shoulder straps also. Generals (including Marshals of Poland) have a silver zigzag embroidered at the end of the shoulder straps, senior officers, two silver stripes, and junior officers, only the stars of rank.

Until 1954 the Polish Army had three generals' ranks, plus that of

Marshal of Poland. The General of Army wore four stars from 1954 to 1958, when finally this rank was abolished. In the early 1950s the three-star rank (General), which still exists, applied to the generals of the corps and services.

During and after the War the ranks were those used in 1939, except for the rank of Warrant Officer which became an officers' rank in 1943 in order to keep in line with the three lieutenants' ranks of the Red Army. When the warrant officers' ranks were readopted in 1963 the one-star officer disappeared; thus at present the 2nd Lieutenant wears two stars.

The rank badges worn on the field cap and on the beret are similar to those worn on the shoulder straps. The generals wear stars above a small zigzag and the officers, stars above double bars, or stars alone, on the left side of the head-dress.

The Marshal of Poland always wears the crossed batons instead of the stars.

Plate 19. Warrant Officers' and N.C.O.s' Rank Badges

The sergeants and corporals wore the pre-war silver lace with red edging until 1961, when a new all-silver lace was introduced. Both ranks still have their badges on the shoulder straps in the form of chevrons and stripes.

As the officers became more academically qualified, the reinstatement of the warrant officers' ranks became necessary. Thus the Warrant Officer and Senior Warrant Officer were created in 1963 and another three W.O.s' ranks were added in 1967. They all have a silver stripe worn all around the loose sides of the shoulder straps and stars from one to four; the junior W.O. wears a star above one chevron.

In 1967 another three sergeants' ranks were added to the existing ones and their rank titles were changed as well.

Plate 20. Rank Badges

The corporals also changed their stripes to the new all-silver lace in 1961 and later, in 1970, a new rank was added, that of Platoon Sergeant, with four stripes.

Collar Patches (1949–52)

New dress regulations, introduced in 1949, dealt with the army collar patches which, with the exception of the armoured troops, were still worn on the collar of the khaki tunic. Personnel of the armoured units by then wore jackets with open collar without any patches. The new collar patches continued to be made in the usual shape in order to fit the pointed collar of the tunic and all ranks wore them with the traditional zigzag as they did before the war. Only the generals' and officers' pattern of embroidery have been illustrated on the first two collar patches; the other patches should be considered simply as a colour guide. The sergeants had a 5-mm zigzag embroidered in silver and the other ranks' zigzag consisted of a 5-mm. stripe of silver lace. The patches were dark carmine with a narrow stripe of arm-of-service colour at the outer end.

The colours were as follows:

	Patch	*Piping*
Infantry	dark carmine	dark blue
Artillery	dark carmine	emerald-green
Engineers	dark carmine	black
Signals	dark carmine	royal blue
Legal Service	dark carmine	light carmine
Quartermaster Service	dark carmine	cornflower-blue
Administrative Service	dark carmine	brown
Medical Service	dark carmine	violet
Veterinaries	dark carmine	grey
Motor Transport Service	dark carmine	silver

The chaplains were all officers and did not wear collar patches. They had the officer's zigzag embroidered on the collar and a plain cross in the corner between the embroidery.

The two colours, dark carmine and the arm-of-service colour, were also worn on the collar of the greatcoat in the form of two 5-mm. stripes, the former at the bottom, the other above it.

These new patches were adopted by regulations published on 1 March 1949, which became compulsory only after 1 January 1951, and the old uniforms could still continue to be worn until the end of that year.

The colours of the collar patches of the internal security forces were not affected by these regulations and the Internal Security Corps continued wearing the dark blue collar patches. Frontier Defence units wore light green triangular pennons with a dark blue stripe, adopted on 1 May 1946.

No collar patches were worn on the field uniform.

Plate 21. Collar Patches for Marshal of Poland and Generals (1952–60)

Collar patches of an entirely new shape were introduced in 1952 for the newly-adopted jackets with open collar; the pointed patches were still worn on the tunic. All the generals, with the exception of those of armoured and mechanised units and of the Warsaw Division, had light carmine patches with piping in the arm-of-service colours. These colours were as follows:

	Patch	*Piping*
Infantry	light carmine	dark blue
1st Warsaw Inf. Div.	yellow	dark blue
Armoured/Mechanised Units	black	light carmine
Artillery/Ordnance	light carmine	Nile-green
Engineers/Mot. Transport	light carmine	black
Signals	light carmine	cornflower-blue
Quartermaster/Admin. Service	light carmine	sky-blue
Medical Service	light carmine	violet
Veterinaries	light carmine	grey
Legal Service	light carmine	scarlet

The Marshal of Poland wore light carmine patches without piping, with the silver eagle clutching the crossed batons embroidered in the centre. The generals had only the eagle embroidered on their patches.

Collar Patches for Officers and Other Ranks (1952–60)

All the officers and other ranks wore the same collar patches between 1952 and 1960: personnel of the armoured and mechanised units wore black patches with dark carmine piping and the rest of the army had dark carmine patches. The different branches of service were distinguished one from the other by metal badges which were pinned onto the patches. The cadets wore tunics with buttoned-up pointed collars: thus they had different-shaped patches, black for armour and dark carmine for the rest of the army. They wore coloured shoulder straps as well.

Collar Badges

These were the collar badges worn by officers and other ranks on the collar patches between 1952 and 1960 and later on their own, pinned on the lapels of the jacket. They were made of white metal (nickel-plated brass), except that of the Medical Service which was made of brass, in order to distinguish it from the white metal badge of the Veterinary Service.

Only the badges for Armoured/Mechanised units, the Administrative, Medical and Veterinary Services and the Construction Battalions, were worn in pairs.

Plate 22. Collar Badges (1961–73)

By 1960 the collar patches were abolished altogether and later new collar badges were adopted. The embroidered eagles of the Marshal of Poland and generals remained basically the same, whilst most of the other badges were changed, and some new ones were added as well.

The Armoured units and the Mechanised units each obtained their own badges and the same applies to the personnel of the Medical and Veterinary Services. The chaplains, who previously wore only the cross, now wear a cross surrounded by a wreath of laurel. Only the badges of the Infantry, the Artillery and the Legal Service remained more or less the same.

The edelweiss of the Mountain Troops is worn as a feather holder, on the hat, and on the collar of the cape.

Shoulder-Strap Badges

All cadets of the Officers' School wear the letters 'SO' on the shoulder straps: the badge of the 1st was introduced in 1952 and subsequently modified in 1961. The badge for cadets at the N.C.O.s' School (*Szkoła Podoficerska*) was also adopted in 1961 but later a new badge was adopted for the N.C.O.s and cadets of the Regular Army, and also another badge for the Warrant Officers' School.

The Polish title of the Army Technical Academy is *Wojskowa Akademia Techniczna*; hence the letters 'WAT' on the badge. The letters 'WAM' on the badge of the Army Medical Academy refer to the Polish title *Wojskowa Akademia Medyczna*. The letters 'SW' stand for *Studium Wojskowe*.

The three remaining badges, illustrated at the bottom of the plate, were adopted some years later and are currently in use.

Plate 23. Breast Pocket Badges for Exemplary Service

The Exemplary Service badges were granted to meritorious other ranks and were worn on the right breast pocket of the jacket. They are made of white metal and coloured enamel, and the ears of wheat on the sides are painted gold.

These badges were introduced in 1951, one for each branch of service, and the first on the left, with the spread eagle in its centre, was introduced in 1953 for personnel who could not qualify for any of the others. The Infantry badges have a red background, Artillery badges have a green background, Armour and Engineers a black background and all branches of the Quartermaster Service have badges with a light blue background.

In 1958 the Driver's badge was awarded in three classes and later an Exemplary Service badge was also instituted for Miners.

Arm Badges

The Polish Marines are part of the Army and therefore they wear army uniforms but have a white metal fouled anchor on the lower left sleeve. The personnel of the Coastal Defence units wear a light blue beret and an arm badge of the same colour depicting an anchor surrounded by a wreath.

The badge of the Regular N.C.O.s' School is embroidered and it is worn on the left arm.

Plate 24. Breast Badges

The badge of the 1st Warsaw Infantry Division is made of white metal and coloured enamels and was adopted soon after the war to commemorate the victorious march from Lenino to Berlin. In its centre there is a portrait of Tadeusz Kościuszko, after whom the Division is named.

The first Grunwald badges were made in bronze, but later others were made in white metal. A smaller replica of this badge is the centrepiece of the Brotherhood of Arms badge, adopted in 1963. The personnel of the Frontier Defence Units and of the 1st Warsaw Cavalry Division wore their own special breast badges made in metal and coloured enamel. The Frontier Defence badge has been adopted recently, while the other is a wartime badge. The meaning of the letters 'WOP' has already been given in the previous pages, whilst the lettering on the badge of the cavalry division stands for *Warszawska Dywizja Kawalerii*.

A number of different badges of schools and training establishments have been worn since 1945. For instance, there are twelve variations of the Officers' School badge, with different lettering at the top as listed below:

OSP	*Oficerska Szkoła Piechoty* Officers' School of Infantry
OSA	*Oficerska Szkoła Artylerii* Officers' School of Artillery
OSAPlot	*Oficerska Szkoła Artylerii Przeciwlotniczej* Officers' School of A.A. Artillery
OSI	*Oficerska Szkoła Inżynierii* Officers' School of Engineers
OSL	*Oficerska Szkoła Łączności* Officers' School of Signals
OSK	*Oficerska Szkoła Kwatermistrzowska* Officers' School of Quartermasters
OSU	*Oficerska Szkoła Uzbrojenia* Officers' School of Ordnance
OSPW	*Oficerska Szkoła Polityczno-Wychowawcza* Political-Educational Officers' School
OSWS	*Oficerska Szkoła Wojsk Samochodowych* Officers' School of Motor Transport
OSBP	*Oficerska Szkoła Broni Pancernej* Officers' School of the Armoured Corps

The two remaining badges, with 'OSL' and 'OSMW' lettered at the top, are those of the Air Force and Naval Officers' Schools. One single school trained both the cadets of the Armoured Corps and of the Motor Transport (*Oficerska Szkoła Broni Pancernej i Wojsk Samochodowych*) but the two courses had different badges.

These badges were all adopted between 1947 and 1950 and in 1953 they were superseded by the diamond-shaped badges shown at the bottom of the plate. The badges of the academies had a white enamel background, those of the schools a red background, and most were named after Polish national heroes and military leaders. The lettering on each badge stands for the branch of service title, as follows:

ASG	*Akademia Sztabu Generalnego* General Staff Academy (Gen. K. Świerczewski's)
WAP	*Wojskowa Akademia Polityczna* Army Political Academy (F. Dzierżyński's)
WAT	*Wojskowa Akademia Techniczna* Army Technical Academy (J. Dąbrowski's)
WAM	*Wojskowa Akademia Medyczna* Army Medical Academy
FWM	*Fakultet Wojskowo – Medyczny* Army Medical Faculty
OSWZ	*Oficerska Szkoła Wojsk Zmechanizowanych* Mechanised Units Officers' School (T. Kościuszko's)
OSWPanc	*Oficerska Szkoła Wojsk Pancernych* Armoured Units Officers' School (S. Czarnecki's)
OSA	*Oficerska Szkoła Wojsk Rakietowych i Artylerii* Rockets and Artillery Officers' School (Gen. J. Bem's)
OSWOPL	*Oficerska Szkoła Wojsk Obrony Przeciwlotniczej* A.A. Defence Officers' School (M. Kalinowski's)
OSI	*Oficerska Szkoła Wojsk Inżynieryjnych* Engineer Officers' School (J. Jasiński's)
OSUZBR	*Oficerska Szkoła Uzbrojenia* Ordnance Officers' School (Lt W. Baginski's and 2nd Lt A. Wieczorkiewicz's)
OSL	*Oficerska Szkoła Łaczności* Signals Officers' School (B. Kowalski's)
OSWOPch	*Oficerska Szkoła Wojsk Chemicznych* Army Chemical Officers' School (S. Ziaj's)
OSS	*Oficerska Szkoła Samochodowa* Motor Transport Officers' School (Gen. A. Waszkiewicz's)
OSR	*Oficerska Szkoła Radiotechniczna* Radio-Technical Officers' School (Capt. S. Bartosik's)
OSWOP	*Oficerska Szkoła Wojsk Ochrony Pogranicza* Frontier Defence Units Officers' School
OSKBW	*Oficerska Szkoła Korpusu Bezpieczeństwa Wewnętrznego* Army Security Officers' School (M. Nowotka's)
OSP	*Oficerska Szkoła Piechoty* Infantry Officers' School

A white enamel badge with the lettering 'W S M W' was also introduced for the Naval Academy and another two badges, both made of brass and red enamel, for the Air Force, one with the letters 'T S W L' and the other with the letters 'O S L'.

On 30 October 1958 new Exemplary Service badges were adopted to replace those illustrated in the preceding plate. They are granted to the other ranks and are worn on the right breast pocket. There are two grades of the same badge, silver and bronze. Later, the silver (white metal) badge was awarded in three classes, shown by numerals on the badge itself.

The wing-shaped badge of a Driver-Mechanic of Tanks and Self-Propelled Guns is also worn on the right breast pocket and it is awarded in four classes. The badge of the top class has an 'M' in the shield, the others have numerals from 1 to 3. It was instituted in 1960.

The keen soldier, in certain cases, can also be awarded the Inventiveness —Improvement badge, in silver after three successful projects, and in gold for five or more projects.

The qualified parachutists wear their badge with the number of jumps in the wreath. The parachute instructors wear the same badge but with a gold wreath. The badge of the 13th International Brigade is worn by ex-members of that Brigade, which was raised in Spain during the Civil War.

Plate 25. Arm Badges
6th POMORSKA Airborne Division

A number of badges have been worn by the personnel of the Division although the round badge last on the right is the divisional badge.

Specialists

These embroidered badges are worn on the left upper sleeve. The numbers, from 1 to 3, show the specialist class of the wearer.

U.S.A.

The United States is a relatively young nation, formed in 1783 by the union of thirteen North-American states, formerly British colonies. A long period of territorial expansion and internal reassessment followed until at the turn of the last century the U.S.A. began to be involved in European affairs. By the end of World War 2 it had become one of the most powerful nations in the world and American troops were stationed on all the world's continents.

The soldier wore different uniforms for different duties and those worn during the latter period of the war were kept in use until the 1950s. He has an elegant appearance, wearing well-tailored uniforms made with good material and embellished by colourful badges. A peaked cap or forage cap, blouse and trousers, all made of khaki material, were usually worn in temperate climates whilst the summer uniform, which is still in use, consisted of a head-dress, shirt and trousers made of a lighter, sandy yellow material. The same shirt was worn with both uniforms, with the same tie, which was usually darker.

On 1 July 1957 the Army Green uniform replaced the old khaki one: it is composed of a head-dress, jacket with open collar and four patch pockets, and trousers made of a greyish-green material.

Currently officers and warrant officers are also required to own the Army Blue uniform for wear on appropriate occasions; it is similar in style to the A.G. uniform, consisting of a peaked cap, jacket and trousers. The jacket and trousers of the generals' uniform are both made of the same blue cloth while the officers and warrant officers wear lighter blue trousers. Special short shoulder straps with insignia of rank on branch colours are worn on the blue uniform (Plate 27), together with cuff stripes, ornamented cap bands and stripes on the trousers, respectively double gold lace stripes for generals and a single stripe, $1\frac{1}{2}$ in. in width, for the others.

The Army White is an optional uniform, identical in style with the A.G. uniform but made of white material.

The Army Blue or White Mess uniforms are also authorised for optional wear by officers and warrant officers. The former is all made of blue cloth (with lighter blue trousers for officers and W.O.s), while the latter is composed of a white peaked cap, jacket and waistcoat, together with black trousers. The peaked caps used with the mess uniforms are the same as worn with the Army Blue and Army White uniforms.

The short jackets have shoulder cords and the rank insignia are on the cuffs, gold oak leaves and stars for the generals, and gold stripes and loops for the officers, with the insignia of branch in between. 2nd Lieutenants and W.O.s do not wear shoulder cords. The blue jackets have lapels with branch colour facings, and the metal-enamel insignia centred upon them, on both sides. A cummerbund is worn instead of a waistcoat. The blue trousers have gold lace stripes, as prescribed for the Army Blue uniform.

The Army Evening Dress is another optional uniform which consists of the peaked cap, jacket and trousers of the Army Blue Mess uniform worn with full dress shirt with wing collar, white bow tie and white waistcoat. A similar dress uniform but with a tail coat was worn officially until 1969 and will be optional until 1 July 1975.

Branches and corps of the Army have official colours which appear as piping on uniform components, in facings, and in the blue and white dress uniforms. They are:

Adjutant General's Corps	dark blue piped with scarlet
Armor	yellow
Army Medical Department	maroon piped with white
Artillery	scarlet
Chaplains	black
Chemical Corps	cobalt-blue piped with golden yellow
Civil Affairs U.S.A.R.	purple piped with white
Corps of Engineers	scarlet piped with white
Military Police Corps	green piped with yellow
Finance Corps	silver grey piped with golden-yellow
Infantry	light blue
Inspector General	dark blue piped with light blue
Military Intelligence	oriental blue piped with silver-grey
Judge Advocate General's Corps	dark blue piped with white
National Guard Bureau	dark blue
Ordnance Corps	crimson piped with yellow
Permanent Professors of United States Military Academy	scarlet piped with silver-grey
Quartermaster Corps	buff
Signal Corps	orange piped with white
Staff Specialist, U.S.A.R.	green
Transportation Corps	brick-red piped with golden-yellow
Women's Army Corps	old gold and moss-tone green
Warrant Officers	brown
Unassigned to Branch	teal-blue piped with white

Plate 26. Cap Badges

The peaked cap and the forage cap are the principal head-dresses worn by all personnel of the U.S. Army, although soft caps, fur caps and helmets are used as well for particular duties or in particular climates. Berets are worn by personnel of the Special Forces.

The eagle from the coat of arms of the United States of America is worn by officers and enlisted men on the peaked cap; on its own by the former and on a brass disc by the latter. The warrant officers have a different badge, depicting a different eagle, clutching two arrows, surrounded by a wreath of laurel.

Generals and field grade officers have gold-embroidered oak leaves on the visor of the ordinary service caps, while all the others have plain black leather visors. The peaked cap of the Army Blue uniform shows the wearer's rank on the cap band as well. Generals have gold-embroidered oak leaves on the blue cap band as well as on the visor, while all officers have gold stripes on the cap band. Field grade officers only have gold oak leaves on the visor; other officers have a plain leather visor. Warrant officers wear a plain visor with only one stripe on the cap band.

The officers' and warrant officers' chin strap is covered with gold wire lace, whilst that of the enlisted men is made of black leather, matching the visor.

The American Eagle is now also worn by all personnel of the Women's Army Corps: the officers wear a cap badge a little smaller than that of the male officers and the W.A.C. enlisted women wear the same badge, but surrounded by a metal ring.

Officers' and warrant officers' rank badges are worn on the left side of the forage cap, known as a garrison cap, and the piping around the top edge of the curtain shows rank distinction as well.

Generals wear gold piping, all other officers wear gold and black piping, warrant officers silver and black piping and enlisted men, piping of their branch of service colour.

Special Forces Insignia

The Special Forces originate from the Special Warfare Center at Fort Bragg, N.C. In June 1960 the U.S. Army activated the 1st Special Forces which assumed the heritage and honours of the wartime 1st Special Forces and of the Ranger battalions. It also became the parent unit for the 1st, 7th and 10th Special Forces Groups (Airborne) stationed respectively at Okinawa, North Carolina and Bad Tölz (Germany).

The 10th Special Forces Group (Airborne) was raised in June 1952 and in September 1953 the 77th was raised from personnel drafted from the 10th, then to be transferred to Germany. In June 1960 the 77th S.F.G.A. was renumbered the 7th and from the spring of 1961 until October 1962 the Group was deployed in Laos under the operational control of the Military Assistance Advisory Group. Several other groups have been raised and many different beret flashes have been adopted since then.

All ranks of the Special Forces wear the green beret and on the beret, their unit's flash, which is a coloured shield, generally woven, on which the officers have the rank badge and the other ranks have the distinctive insignia of the Special Forces, illustrated at top left. The distinctive insignia on the right is that of the Special Warfare Center.

The first flashes adopted were yellow, red, green and blue and some were later modified: for instance, a black border to commemorate J. F. Kennedy's death was added to the yellow flash of the 1st, and the German national colours were added to the flash of the 10th S.F.G.A. – Europe, stationed in Germany. The colours of the South Vietnamese flag are on the flash of the 5th S.F.G.A. from which the 5th Combat Assistance developed, with a flash of its own. The U.S. Advisors in Cambodia, a training group, wore a flash similar in design to the latter: it is dark blue with golden yellow border, with three white stars on red background at the top left and a white silhouette on the right.

The 3rd S.F.G.A. was formed by personnel of the 1st, 5th and 7th, and the yellow, black and red colours of its parent units are part of its flash. The Special Forces Aviation and the Special Warfare Center, named after President Kennedy, have their own flashes, and also wear particular shoulder patches (Plates 32 and 34) differing from the arrowhead patch of the Special Forces (Plate 34).

Plate 27. Officers' Rank Badges

In the U.S. Army silver rank badges have seniority over gold ones; for instance in the case of the badges of Lieutenant Colonel and Major and those of lieutenants. They were all adopted during the last century except for the generals' stars which were adopted some time earlier. Initially, the U.S. Army had only two generals' ranks: Brigadiers and Major Generals. The rank of Lieutenant General was instituted in 1799 and from that year to 1802 the rank of General of the Armies of the United States existed as well and was later conferred on John J. Pershing in 1919. The rank of General of the Army was instituted in 1866 and once again in 1944.

The officers' rank badges are usually worn on the shoulder straps of the jacket and overcoat or on the right side of the shirt collar when the jacket is not worn. They are also worn on the left side of the garrison cap and on the head-dress of the field and work uniforms.

These badges are made of metal or are embroidered in metal wire; machine-embroidered or woven rank badges are usually worn on field and work uniforms.

Warrant Officers' Rank Badges

Brass and enamel bars with rounded ends became the rank badges of the

Warrant Officer and of the Chief Warrant Officer in 1942 but, some years after the Korean War, in 1956, two new ranks were instituted. Thus there are now one warrant officer rank (W1) and three chief warrant officer ranks (W2, 3 and 4). The rank badges were changed to rectangular bars with three enamel blocks for CWO4 and CWO2 and only two enamel blocks for CWO3 and WO1; the bars of the two top ranks were made of white metal whilst those of the two lower ranks were made of brass.

As these badges caused a great deal of visual confusion, new badges have been adopted since 1 December 1972. The new badges are all made of white metal with black enamel blocks, one for each warrant rank. There are also subdued versions for field and work uniforms.

Shoulder Ornamentation for Army Blue Uniform

On the Army Blue uniform the rank badges are embroidered on special rectangular straps, previously used on blue uniforms during the last century. The straps are surrounded by a gold nylon or rayon border, $\frac{3}{8}$-in. in width with a single line of gold Jaceron on either side. The strap background is of blue-black velvet for generals and, for officers, of cloth in the branch-of-service colours. If the branch of service has two colours the first named colour constitutes the background and the second replaces the inner line of Jaceron. The warrant officers have a brown background.

The generals and the colonels wear one set of stars or, respectively, one eagle for each strap, whilst the other officers and warrant officers wear one badge on each side of the shoulder strap.

Plate 28. Line N.C.O.s' Rank Badges (1948)

The American N.C.O.s wore the wartime chevrons (80 mm. in width) until 1948, when both the ranks and the rank badges were changed. The technician (T) ranks were all abolished and the three-chevron ranks of (Buck) Sergeant were abolished as well. The new badges adopted in 1948 were considerably smaller (48 mm. in width) and were woven, the same as the shoulder sleeve insignia. Combatant personnel wore blue chevrons on a yellow background and non-combatant personnel wore yellow chevrons on dark blue.

The American N.C.O.s' ranks are related to their pay grade which until 1948 went from E-1 (M/Sgt and 1st Sgt) to E-7 (Soldier). In 1948 the succession of pay grade was inverted, i.e. the M/Sgt and the 1st Sgt became the seventh enlisted man pay grade.

1955

In 1955 larger chevrons (80 mm. in width) were once again introduced for the line N.C.O.s' ranks together with four new specialists' ranks. The chevrons of the former were machine-embroidered in khaki silk on a dark blue gabardine material; those of the specialists were considerably smaller (50 mm. in width) with the American Eagle embroidered in the centre

1957–73
When the new Army Green uniforms were adopted in 1957, new yellow chevrons were adopted as well for both the line N.C.O.s and the specialists (Plate 29) and several new ranks were introduced in the following years.

The following were the ranks in use until 1958:

Pay Grade	Line N.C.O.s	Technicians
E-7	First Sergeant	Master Specialist
	Master Sergeant	
E-6	Sergeant 1st Class	Specialist 1st Class
E-5	Sergeant	Specialist 2nd Class
E-4	Corporal	Specialist 3rd Class
E-3	Private 1st Class	none
E-2	Private	none
E-1	Recruit – under four months' service	none

In 1958, the three-chevron rank of Sergeant (E-5) was re-introduced and the former rank of Sergeant, with four chevrons, became that of Staff Sergeant (E-6). As a result the pay grade was pushed forward one grade all along the line and a new rank, that of Sergeant Major (E-9), was created, with six chevrons and a star.

On 1 September 1965, a wreath was added around the star on the rank badge of the Sergeant Major and his previous badge, with six chevrons and the star, was taken on by the new rank of Chief Master Sergeant, which was re-titled Staff Sergeant Major in 1968 and Sergeant Major on 1 July 1969. The chevrons with the star and wreath became the badge of the Command Sergeant Major in 1968. Both these two N.C.O.s' ranks belong to the E-9 pay grade.

Another E-9 rank is that of Sergeant Major of the Army, created in July 1966. This rank is covered by a single man serving at the Pentagon who wears on the sleeves the chevrons of the Command Sergeant Major, plus special brass and enamel collar badges.

A new rank badge consisting of one chevron with another round one below was adopted in 1965 for the new Lance Corporal rank (E-3) and the Private 1st Class took the E-2 pay grade. Later, in 1968, the Lance Corporal became a Private 1st Class (E-3) and the one-chevron rank was renamed Private E-2.

The Platoon Sergeant wears the same chevrons as the Sergeant 1st Class and both ranks belong to the E-7 pay grade.

Plate 29. Specialists' Rank Badges (1956 and 1958)

New specialists' ranks were adopted in 1955 represented by badges embroidered in yellow on greyish-green gabardine material. The lowest specialist's class corresponded to the line N.C.O.'s rank of Corporal and to the E-4 pay grade.

The specialist's rank and rank badges were changed in 1958. New larger rank badges were adopted and the specialists were named after their corresponding pay grade number. Until 1968, however, all the specialists were technically subordinated to the line N.C.O. of the rank of Corporal, while since June of that year they have been subordinated to the line N.C.O. of identical pay grade and above the N.C.O. of the lower pay grade.

The ranks of Specialists 8 and 9 have never been worn.

Shoulder Sleeve Tabs

Traditionally the U.S. Army did not use shoulder tabs as a means of unit recognition. The Ranger battalions, however, wore the familar numbered scroll tabs during World War 2. Another 'RANGER' tab, with its title in white on a red straight tab, was worn at that time by personnel of the 5th Army. A curved 'RANGER' tab, yellow on black, appeared some years later during the Korean War. It also had the title 'AIRBORNE' below.

Tabs of U.S. Army locations were, and still are, in use. The tab 'KOREA' can also be found with white lettering on blue background. 'KMAG' stands for Korea Military Advisory Group and was worn below the patch of the Military Government of Korea (Plate 33).

The 'INVADERS' tab was worn by the band of SHAEF during the latter stage of the war and some personnel of the 88th Division wore the unofficial scroll tab 'BLUE DEVIL' above the divisional patch. The Division was then stationed in the region of Venezia Giulia, in the North-East of Italy. In 1947 the Free Territory of Trieste was formed, and the 88th Division composed the nucleus of TRUST (Plate 33), the U.S. Army contingent stationed in Trieste. The close relation between the 88th Division and TRUST can be seen in the similarity of both the patches and tabs worn by the two units.

In later years, the raising of Special Forces and Long Range Patrols started an urge for individuality among the units of the U.S. Army, and particularly in the Vietnam theatre of operations dozens of tabs were adopted although most were unofficial.

Divisional and regimental Airborne-Ranger and Pathfinder-Airborne detachments and Long Range patrols were raised and adopted their own self-explanatory tabs which were worn above the shoulder patch. For instance, the scroll tab with 'AIRBORNE-RANGER/INF.CO.' embroidered in white with red edging was worn above the patch of the Americal Division. The letters 'LRRP' stand for Long Range Reconnaissance Patrol and 'RECONDO' for Reconnaissance Commando.

When all the Airborne-Ranger Companies were organised as part of the 75th Infantry Regiment (see Marshall Task Force, Plate 34) the tabs of the companies in Vietnam were standardised, with the company's letter ('A', 'B', 'C', etc.) on the left and '75', the regimental number, on the right. 'AIRBORNE-RANGER' was in the scroll's centre.

The 'AIRBORNE-RANGER' tabs with the company letter were worn on field uniforms while on the ordinary service uniforms an 'AIR-BORNE' tab (white on blue or yellow on black) was added above the patch of wearer's unit, as in the following list:

Abn Ranger Company	Unit
A	197th Inf. Bde
B	7th Corps
C	1st Field Force
D	2nd Field Force
E	9th Inf. Division
F	25th Inf. Division
G	Americal Division
H	1st Cav. Division (Airmobile)
I	1st Inf. Division
K	4th Inf. Division
L	101st Abn Division
M	199th Inf. Bde
N	173rd Abn Bde
O	3/82nd Abn Division
P	5th Inf. Division (Mech.)

Some variations exist, for instance, in the case of L Company, 'CO' and 'INF' are added on the scroll ends, which in this case are square.

The red and black scroll tab 'USSF/SPECIAL TASK FORCE/B-36' was worn on the right shoulder by the Team B-36, 5th Special Forces in Vietnam.

The Tomahawk patch is worn by the 5th Bn, 23rd Infantry Regiment and the motto 'Go Devils' belongs to the 1st Bn, 60th Infantry Regiment of the 172nd Infantry Brigade.

Only a selection of shoulder-sleeve tabs has been illustrated, and many others can be found by the collector, embroidered in various colours or in the subdued black on olive-green variation.

Plate 30. Officers' Collar Badges

The U.S. Army officers wear four badges on the collar and lapels of the jacket: two U.S. national insignia, one for each side, at the top, and the service branch badges at the bottom. On the collar of the summer shirt the rank badge is worn on the right and the branch badge on the left.

The infantry badge illustrated belongs to an officer of the 349th Infantry Regiment, of the 88th Division, and it was worn soon after World War 2.

During the last twenty-eight years several collar badges have been modified in conformity with the Army's reorganisation, and some others have been abolished as the branch of service they represented no longer exists.

The Armored Force adopted a new badge, the design of which links the cavalry with its armoured role, although the cavalry and the tank units still keep their separate identity. Personnel of cavalry units have now readopted the crossed sabres. The use of numerals above the crossed sabres is permitted but not squadron numbers or letters.

In the late 1950s, when missiles became standard equipment of the Artillery, a 'composite missile' was added to the traditional crossed cannons.

The letters attached to the Medical Corps badges were made of brass or maroon enamel, but soon after another pattern, with black letters, was introduced, which is worn currently.

The Aide-de-Camp badges were introduced in 1902, initially for Aides to Brigadier, Major and Lieutenant General; in 1918 the badge for General's Aide was adopted, with four stars in the chief.

These early devices were entirely different from the later types: they were slightly larger, as it was only in 1921 that their height was standardised at $1\frac{1}{4}$ in. and until 1924 the stars were made of gold. The shield of early badges was convex and its top edge was usually straight. Some shields had pointed upper corners, others were with the eagle's wings overlapping onto the corners of the shield. As the latter type appeared in the U.S. Marine Corps regulations, it is technically a U.S.M.C. badge, although often used by Army personnel as well.

Both types were also made in bronze and smaller Aides' badges were worn on the shirt collar. Other types were embroidered respectively on dark brown or khaki, olive-drab, olive-green and white material. Subdued badges are made of black silk on olive-green.

The badge for Aide to the General of the Army was adopted in 1944, and in 1951 a round badge was introduced for Aides to the President. Two years later, in May 1953, this badge was replaced by another which conforms to the usual pattern. In May 1969 a similar badge, but with inverted colours of enamel, was approved for the Aide to the Vice President.

In 1951, badges for the Aides to the Secretary of Defense and Secretary of the Army were also introduced and in February 1963 those for Aides to the Under-Secretary of the Army and to the Chief of Staff.

The coat of arms of the latter is superimposed on a white star. The arm and service badges worn by enlisted men are similar to those of the officers, but entirely made of brass and superimposed on a brass disc.

Plate 31. Breast Badges

The Department of Defense Identification badge, known at present as the Office of the Secretary of Defense Identification badge, is worn on the left pocket by individuals who have served not less than one year, after 13 January 1961, in the Office of the Secretary of Defense.

The Presidential Service badge was instituted on 1 June 1961 and it is awarded to individuals who have served for not less than one year at the White House. It is worn on the right breast pocket.

The Joint Chiefs of Staff Identification badge is worn on the left pocket by individuals who have served not less than one year in the organisation.

The Army General Staff Identification badge is the oldest badge of this type as it was authorised on 23 October 1933 for officers who, since 1920, had served for not less than one year on the General Staff. It is worn on the right pocket.

The Guard, Tomb of the Unknown Soldier, Identification badge is worn on the right breast pocket by members of the Honor Guard in Washington, D.C.

The Expert Infantryman and the Combat Infantryman badges are made of silver and blue enamel and are worn above the ribbons; the former is awarded to infantrymen who have satisfactorily completed a number of proficiency tests, the other is awarded for meritorious combat performance. The Combat Artillery and Armored Cavalry badges are unofficial.

There are three classes of parachutists' badges: the Master Parachutist badge is awarded for sixty-five jumps, including twenty-five with combat equipment, four at night and five mass tactical jumps: the wearer must be a qualified 'jumpmaster' or have served as jumpmaster on at least one combat jump or thirty-three non-combat jumps.

The badge of Senior Parachutist is awarded after thirty jumps, including fifteen with combat equipment, two at night and two mass tactical jumps. The wearer must be a qualified jumpmaster or have taken part in one or more combat jumps or fifteen non-combat jumps as a jumpmaster.

The Master and Senior Parachutists must have served on jump status for respectively thirty-six and twenty-four months.

All the other army-qualified parachutists wear the winged parachute illustrated, worn above the unit's identification oval. Ranger-qualified parachutists wear the same badge with the Ranger tab.

The Glider badge is no longer awarded, but it is still worn by those who have qualified for it.

There are three types of Army Aviation badges in existence, each divided into three classes: the plain wings, the wings surmounted by a star, and the badge with the star surrounded by a wreath. The badges are worn respectively by the Master and Senior Army Aviator and by the Army Aviator; by the Senior Flight Surgeon, Flight Surgeon and Aviation Medical Officer; and by the Master, Senior and Aircraft Crewman.

There are four badges for nuclear reactor operators, awarded to graduates of the Nuclear Power Plant Operators Course, and after periods of such duty. The Reactor Commander badge and the Shift Supervisor badge are identical but the former is worn by officers. There are also the Operator First and Second Class badges and the Operator Basic badge.

The Explosive Ordnance Disposal Specialist and the Supervisor wear similar badges, that of the latter with a star.

Medical personnel wear the Expert Field Medical badge after completion of proficiency tests whilst the Combat Medical badges are worn by personnel who have satisfactorily performed their duty on active ground combat.

Plate 32. Shoulder Sleeve and Pocket Insignia

Coloured patches are worn by army personnel on the upper sleeves of the jacket and overcoat and on the shirt when it is worn as an outer garment. The same patches, but of the subdued type (black and olive-green), are worn on field work and other utility uniforms. They come in two versions, woven or machine-embroidered in black on an olive-green cloth.

All personnel wear the patch of the unit in which they currently serve on the left upper sleeve. Individuals who have earned merit in combat operations during World War 2 (7 December 1941 – 2 September 1946), the Korean War (27 June 1950 – 27 July 1954), in Korea after 1 April 1968, in Vietnam after 1 July 1958 and in the Dominican Republic after 29 April 1965, are entitled to wear the patch of the unit they belonged to at that time on the right upper sleeve.

A great number of coloured and subdued patches are also worn on one of the breast pockets of field and utility uniforms.

Most patches are currently woven, or partly woven on felt, although others have been hand-embroidered in the Far East, particularly in Vietnam.

Several units retain the badge they wore during World War 2 but even the woven badges made nowadays are considerably different from the old ones. Before the adoption of the Army Green uniforms many patches used to have a khaki background or a narrow khaki border; these backgrounds are now Army Green and many patches are now made with a thick woven coloured border.

Recruiting and Training

The U.S. Army Recruiting Service initially had a shield-shaped patch, later changed to an oval one, with the Liberty Bell surrounded by the stars of the first thirteen states of the Union.

The Armed Forces Information School existed in the late 1940s and early 1950s at the Carlisle Barracks, Pa, and the three stars in the patch symbolised the Army, Navy and U.S.A.F., which it served. The Army Aviation School is located at Fort Rucker, Ala. The Helicopter School, whose pocket patch is illustrated below, is part of the Army Aviation School.

The Psychological Warfare Division was established in 1950 at the Army General School at Fort Riley, Kansas. Two years later it was transferred to Fort Bragg, N.C., and it became the Psychological Warfare Center, renamed the Special Warfare Center in December 1956. This establishment is dedicated to President J. F. Kennedy.

The Jungle Warfare Training Center was created in 1951 at Fort Sherman, Panama Canal Zone, and in May 1960 it became an independent command under the U.S. Army, Caribbean.

Centers and Schools

The first patch of the Field Artillery School depicted a cannon only but when, later, it became the Artillery and Missile School the black missile was added to the patch. In July 1970 a third patch was adopted, without the missile but of a different design from the first one. Similar diamond-shaped patches were adopted for the Training Commands of the various branches of service, and later they were all renamed Center and School (i.e. Missile and Munitions Center and School, etc.).

Four patches of Recondo (Reconnaissance Commando) Schools have been illustrated among others at the bottom of the plate. They are only a selection as many others are in existence and all are usually in the shape of an arrowhead. Company G, 75th Infantry Regiment, was the Recondo unit of the American (23rd) Division, and Company P was raised by the 5th Division. The other two are patches of independent Recondo units raised respectively in Hawaii and by the U.S. Military Academy.

The Imjin Scout insignia is worn as a pocket patch by personnel and graduates of the Advance Combat Training Academy of 2nd Division, stationed near the Demilitarised Zone in Korea. It is also worn below a 'SNIPER' tab and on armbands worn on the left sleeve by personnel of the DMZ Police. Patches exist with and without the letters 'DMZ' at the bottom, below the map of Korea.

The 54th Engineers Professional School, previously a battalion, has now been renamed 130th Engineers Brigade Professional School.

The full title of the first patch on the fifth row is Combat Surveillance Electronic School.

Plate 33. Shoulder Sleeve and Pocket Insignia
U.S. Forces Overseas

The shoulder patch of the U.S. Army, Europe, is similar to the patch of the former Supreme Headquarters Allied Expeditionary Force, except that its background is now blue, instead of black. The same patch with the word 'BERLIN' as part of the patch, at the top, was adopted by the U.S. troops stationed in Berlin. The U.S. troops stationed in Trieste from 1947 to 1953 wore a modified patch of the 88th Division, to which they used to belong, with the halberd of the town of Trieste in its centre and an additional self-explanatory scroll. Some patches of the Tactical Command, Austria, can also be found with two scrolls, one at the top, similar in shape to that of the 'TRUST' with the inscription 'AUSTRIA' and another at the bottom which reads 'LINZ'.

The U.S. Forces in Austria used to wear a patch made in the Austrian colours, with a sword and a twig of laurel in its centre. The patch of the U.S. Forces, Far East, depicts Mount Fujiyama and later, with an additional scroll, it became the badge of the 29th R.C.T. (Plate 36). A Torii gate is depicted on the shoulder patch of the Ryukyus Command, with its headquarters at Okinawa. The U.S. personnel in Guam have in turn worn two different badges. Both have been illustrated.

The fleurs-de-lis are present on the badge of the U.S. TASCOM, Europe, because this organisation was originally formed on 25 April 1953 in France; the central arrow represents the flow of supplies. On 6 August 1964 it was renamed U.S. Army Communications Zone, Europe, and on 26 September 1969 it became the U.S. Theater Army Support Command, Europe. Similar logistical organisations were also set up in Japan and Korea and wore their own patches. They were later organised as part of a network of logistical commands, whose patches are illustrated on Plate 39.

A number of new patches have been adopted in recent years by units in Vietnam, and by the various Military Assistance Advisory Groups and similar organisations raised in the Far East.

The bell-shaped patch of the former Military Government of Korea has a tab fitted at the bottom (Plate 29). The letters 'KMAG' of this tab stand for Korea Military Advisory Group.

Plate 34. Shoulder Sleeve and Pocket Insignia Miscellaneous U.S. Units

The China Headquarters, Ledo Road, the Marshall Task Force and the Jingpaw and Katchin Rangers were all formations which fought the Japanese during World War 2 and most of their shoulder sleeve insignia were worn by veterans after the war, on the right sleeve.

The patch of the Marshall Task Force is very similar except for the tab, to that of the Merrill's Marauders, although it also had another patch with 'MARS TASK FORCE' written in blue, all on one line, on a curved green tab. The same shield, without any tab, became the distinctive insignia of the 75th Infantry Regiment, raised on 5 December 1968 as the parent unit of all the Long Range Reconnaissance Patrol units.

The 75th is descended from the 475th Infantry Regiment which, together with the 24th Cavalry Regiment, 612th and 613th Field Artillery Battalions and a Chinese infantry regiment, formed the 5332nd Brigade (Provisional) then, in 1944, stationed in India. This American formation was first known as Galahad Force, organised on 10 September 1943 and renamed 5307th Composite Unit (Provisional) on 1 January 1944. It was stationed at Camp Deogarth, India, and later, under the command of Brigadier Frank D. Merrill, it was deployed in the recovery of Northern Burma in operations which led to the construction of the Ledo Road, linking the Indian Railway station of Ledo with the Burma Road to China.

The 5332nd Brigade was later sent to China where it was used as a training unit for Chinese troops; the 475th Regiment was disbanded on 1 July 1945. It was reactivated as the 75th Infantry Regiment at Okinawa on 20 November 1954, disbanded on 21 March 1956 and re-raised once again in 1968.

At that time there were twelve L.R.R.P. units in Vietnam which all became companies of the new regiment (Plate 29).

The wings of the Office of Strategic Service Special Force were worn on the right sleeve, halfway between the shoulder and the elbow, by about a hundred Americans attached to the British S.O.E.

There are several variations of the Bushmasters' patches, particularly of the infantry one, as it was originally worn by units stationed in the Panama Canal Zone, later becoming a Regimental Combat Team and subsequently Brigade (Plate 36).

A number of Chemical Mortar Battalions wore shoulder patches during World War 2 and that of the 100th, for instance was hand-embroidered in Italy where the battalion was stationed in 1944. The Training Engineers units have rectangular patches in arm-of-service colours, with the engineers' castle in its centre, and often with the battalion number embroidered above. The Quartermaster Corps badge is depicted on the Quartermasters' patch, on a blue circular background. The winged sword can be seen in the shoulder patch of the Special Category Army With Air Force (SCARWAF), an organisation formed in 1952.

The U.S. Army Alaska Supply Group was previously known as 69th General Support Group, and before that as the U.S. Army Support, Alaska. The Arctic Rangers is also an Alaskan-based unit: its personnel wear the green beret with a Special Forces flash (Plate 26).

Finally, the arrowhead shoulder patch of the Special Forces was worn alternately with two different airborne tabs. The Army Aviation personnel of the S.F.G.A. wear a different self-explanatory patch.

Plate 35. Shoulder Sleeve Insignia
Ghost Units, National Guard Divisions and Miscellanea

A number of shoulder patches, never actually worn on uniform, are commonly known as patches of 'ghost units'. Most are insignia of Infantry and Airborne (Plate 44) divisions whose patches were designed and put into production during World War 2, but the units themselves were never formed.

Some National Guard divisions were activated in the early 1950s and subsequently disbanded, after the Korean War.

Many shoulder insignia have been modified since the end of World War 2: Army Green has replaced khaki in order to match the colour of the uniforms adopted in 1957. In the case of the 89th Infantry Division, whose background was solely khaki, a new coloured patch was adopted altogether. The 40th Infantry Division, known as the 'Ball of Fire', adopted a new patch while serving in Korea.

The original patch of 1st Army was a black 'A' on a khaki background but personnel of the Army's different branches of service had their branch colours added to the patch. A different patch was issued after the War with the 'A' on a white and red background, without additional colours.

The 19th Army Corps used to have a blue and white insignia during the War which subsequently was slightly modified to the pattern illustrated. Special units of some divisions had scrolls, letters or numerals added to their original patches, as in the case of the Honor Guard and Long Range Reconnaissance Patrol of the 5th Infantry Division. A number of modified patches have also been adopted, especially by the 7th, 24th and 25th Infantry Divisions, during spells of active service in the Far East.

The 11th Air Assault (Test) Division was formed on 1 February 1963 and on 3 July 1965 it became the 1st Cavalry Division (Airmobile). As its title suggests, it was an experimental formation whose units tested the new tactic of airborne-helicopter warfare.

Plate 36. Shoulder Sleeve Insignia
Regimental Combat Teams

The Combat Team 442 was a unit raised among Japanese–Americans which fought as an independent formation during World War 2. It is the first regimental team to have its own insignia and, as a matter of fact, its personnel wore two different shoulder patches in turn. The second pattern was also used after the War when the 442nd became a Regimental Combat Team. The 25th R.C.T. also existed during World War 2.

The Regimental Combat Team consisted of an infantry regiment, a field artillery battalion and a company of engineers and services, thus forming a self-supporting fighting unit. Three R.C.T.s formed the Triangular Division of the early 1950s. During the mid 1960s they were gradually replaced by the newly-formed brigades.

There are also two variations of the patch of the 5th R.C.T., one with two crossed rifles and the other with a yellow thunderbolt on the pentagon. A tab was worn as well, with the lettering '5 R.C.T.' in white on a red background bordered white. The latest patch of the 75th R.C.T. was slightly different from that illustrated: the shield was light blue, without the white inner border.

The 103rd R.C.T. was a unit from Maine and the 107th a unit from New York. The shoulder patch of the 111th contains a silhouette of Benjamin Franklin. The black diamond of the 150th symbolises the coal mines of West Virginia and the Mount Rushmore figures are on the patch of the 196th R.C.T.

Personnel of the 187th Airborne R.C.T. have worn about twelve variants, all slightly different, of the same badge, plus two of the three pocket patches illustrated at the bottom of this plate.

The 298th and 299th were Hawaiian units, and the patch of the former shows the face of King Kamehameha I and a Hawaiian spear. The spear and a kahili are depicted on the patch of the other.

The shoulder patch of the 351st R.C.T. is made in the shape of an axe head. The 74th Infantry Regiment was raised during the War and later became the 474th R.C.T. Its badge depicts a blue Viking ship surmounted by a small Ranger scroll, all on a red arrowhead; in some of these badges, however, the positioning of the blue and red have been inverted.

The black and white patch on the bottom row is the pocket patch of the 65th R.C.T., a unit raised in Puerto Rico.

Plate 37. Shoulder Sleeve Insignia
Brigades

All the shoulder sleeve insignia illustrated in this plate belong to Infantry and Artillery brigades, most of which were raised in the 1960s. All information concerning these patches is given below in an abbreviated form.

1st and 2nd Infantry Brigades	Originally part of 1st Inf. Div. Both were transformed to Abn Bdes in the summer of 1943. The 1st was disbanded the following January, the 2nd (Plate 44), in 1945. Both became independent Inf. Bdes in 1958 and in 1962 were returned to 1st Inf. Div.
11th Infantry Brigade	Insignia officially approved on 26 July 1966.
29th Infantry Brigade	Hawaiian N.G. (National Guard). Insignia approved on 9 September 1964 and 16 May 1968.
32nd Infantry Brigade	Insignia of former 32nd Div. Wisconsin N.G. approved for the Inf. Bde on 17 May 1968.
33rd Infantry Brigade	As above, Illinois N.G. 1 July 1968.
36th Infantry Brigade	Texas N.G. Brigade. 10 May 1967.
39th Infantry Brigade	Arkansas N.G. 24 September 1968.
40th Infantry Brigade	Insignia of former 40th Inf. Div. California N.G. readopted on 1 May 1968.
40th Armored Brigade	California N.G. 30 January 1969.
41st Infantry Brigade	12 June 1969.
45th Infantry Brigade	Insignia of former 45th Inf. Div. Oklahoma N.G.
49th Infantry Brigade	California N.G. 4 November 1966.
49th Armored Brigade	Texas N.G.
53rd Infantry Brigade	Florida N.G. Formerly armoured 4 December 1964. An infantry unit since 25 July 1968.
67th Infantry Brigade	Nebraska N.G. 16 June 1964.
69th Infantry Brigade	Kansas N.G. 3 December 1964.
71st Airborne Brigade	Insignia of former 36th Inf. Div. Texas N.G. 10 March 1969.
72nd Infantry Brigade	Texas N.G. 18 September 1968.
81st Infantry Brigade	Washington N.G. Indian symbol of a raven. 27 May 1970.

86th Infantry Brigade	Vermont N.G. 1 July 1964.
92nd Infantry Brigade	Puerto Rico N.G. 16 June 1964.
157th Infantry Brigade	Pennsylvania A.R. 13 July 1964.
171st Infantry Brigade	Alaskan unit. 28 August 1963.
172nd Infantry Brigade	As above.
173rd Airborne Brigade	Also Plate 44. 29 July 1963.
187th Infantry Brigade	Massachusetts A.R. 3 October 1963.
191st Infantry Brigade	24 October 1963.
193rd Infantry Brigade	23 August 1962.
194th Armored Brigade	13 January 1966.
196th Infantry Brigade	Double-headed match for matchlock muskets. 29 October 1965.
197th Infantry Brigade	A cartridge. 14 December 1962.
198th Infantry Brigade	6 July 1967.
199th Infantry Brigade	10 June 1966.
205th Infantry Brigade	A unit of Minnesota. 1 November 1963.
256th Infantry Brigade	Louisiana A.R. 23 July 1968.
30th Artillery Brigade	Raised in the Ryukyus Islands. The three arrows (symbolising missiles) and the circle suggest the Brigade's number. 12 April 1966.
31st, 35th, 45th, 47th, 49th, 52nd Army Air Defense Command (ARADCOM).	
32nd Artillery Brigade	20 April 1966, became ARADCOM with its own patch on 16 July 1966.
38th Artillery Brigade	Insignia suggests the partition of Korea. 2 June 1961.
40th A.A. Artillery Brigade	10 June 1955. Later became part of ARADCOM and in 1971 was redesignated 13th Art. Group.
107th Artillery Brigade	Virginia N.G. 31 May 1967.

The Army Defense Command, divided into regions, secures the anti-aircraft defence of all the territory of the United States.

Plate 38. Shoulder Sleeve Insignia
Brigades

The patches of all the remaining brigades, of Engineers, Ordnance, etc., are illustrated in this plate.

7th Engineers Brigade	The saltire is the map symbol of a brigade. The seven stripes symbolise this Brigade number and red and white are the colours of the Engineers.
16th Engineers Brigade	The Roman number 'X' plus the six merlons on the towers form this Brigade's number. Ohio N.G. 9 July 1968.

155

18th Engineers Brigade	10 February 1966.
20th Engineers Brigade	Four Roman 'V's add up to the Brigade's number. 30 June 1967.
130th Engineers Brigade	23 September 1969.
411th Engineers Brigade	4 January 1967.
412th Engineers Brigade	Mississippi A.R. 8 November 1967. Later a Command.
416th Engineers Brigade	20 April 1967.
420th Engineers Brigade	18 December 1967.
57th Ordnance Brigade	Crimson-yellow patch with central grenade.
1st Signal Brigade	The electric spark combined with the army's sword.
7th Signal Brigade	16 March 1970.
1st Support Brigade	The millrind is a symbol of strength. 11 February 1966.
2nd Support Brigade	The chevrons simulate a belt supporting the sword and symbolise the unit's number. 15 February 1966.
3rd Support Brigade	Three lances supporting each other. 19 August 1966.
12th Support Brigade	2 February 1966.
13 Support Brigade	11 August 1966.
15th Support Brigade	A supporting arch. 19 December 1966.
35th Support Brigade	Insignia of former 35th Inf. Div. 23 July 1969.
103rd Support Brigade	Insignia of former 103rd Inf. Div. 4 January 1967.
167th Support Brigade	Symbolic support to the above combat section. 14 July 1969.
301st Support Brigade	The chain of supply, the chain symbolising strength. 19 January 1966. Formerly a Command since 21 March 1952.
311th Support Brigade	21 March 1968. Formerly a Command since 22 March 1955.
377th Support Brigade	21 September 1966.
15th M.P. Brigade	18 April 1966.
18th M.P. Brigade	The army's sword upon the magistrate's fasces. 1 June 1966.
43rd M.P. Brigade	Rhode Island N.G. Rhodes city walls. 18 May 1969.
220th M.P. Brigade	Located at Gaithersburg, Maryland, an A.R. unit.
221st M.P. Brigade	The griffin head above the Californian Sun. U.S.A.R.
258th M.P. Brigade	Insignia of the former 258th R.C.T. 24 September 1968.

290th M.P. Brigade	Nashville, Tennessee, U.S.A.R.
7th Medical Brigade	21 February 1966.
18th Medical Brigade	Entwined medical bandages. 25 October 1967.
44th Medical Brigade	5 October 1966.
1st Aviation Brigade	Formed in Vietnam. 2 August 1966.
107th Transportation Brigade	11 May 1966.
125th Transportation Brigade	The symbol of water and road transportation.
143rd Transportation Brigade	Roads and viaducts. 24 October 1969.

The 184th and 425th Transportation Commands (Plate 39) have recently been transformed into Brigades.

Plate 39. Shoulder Sleeve Insignia
Logistical Commands

The 1st Logistical Command was activated at Fort McPherson, Georgia, on 20 September 1950 and its patch was authorised on 12 May 1952. The Command was later transferred to Fort Bragg and subsequently to France. Back in the U.S.A., for a time it was part of 3rd Corps at Fort Hood, Texas, and in April 1965 it arrived in Vietnam. It was renamed 1st Field Army Support Command and replaced the 22nd FASCOM at Fort Lee, Virginia.

The 2nd Logistical Command was formed in Korea; thus the map of Korea is depicted in one of its shoulder patches, the Torii gate on the other.

A number of other commands have been formed since the 1950s in order to secure the supplies to the various U.S. Army units and all wear round-shaped shoulder sleeve insignia, 5 cm. in diameter.

A section of the Golden Gate bridge can be recognised on the patch of the 305th, and the silhouette of Morro Castle, in Puerto Rico, on that of the 324th Logistical Command.

Transportation Commands

The Transportation commands' patches show the colour of this branch of service, brick-red and yellow, and most depict wheels. However, a section of a railway track can be seen in the patch of the 3rd and the magnolia flower of Mississippi in that of 184th Transportation Command.

Plate 40. Shoulder Sleeve and Pocket Insignia
Commands

These last few patches illustrated were worn by personnel of commands whose badges could not be included in the previous plates. The 14th A.A. Command, for instance, is the only one of its kind and existed during and after World War 2.

The U.S. Army Investigation Command was organised on 15 September 1971 and is divided into six regions (1st U.S. Army, 3rd U.S. Army, 5th U.S. Army, 6th U.S. Army, U.S. Army Pacific and U.S. Army Europe and Africa), plus several field offices.

The abbreviation 'FASCOM' stands for Field Army Support Command.

Cavalry – Armored and Airmobile

Only the 1st Cavalry Division saw active service during World War 2, although several cavalry units were deployed as independent armoured regiments or groups. In 1965 the 1st Cavalry Division became 'airmobile', thus adding another role to the cavalry. The great majority of the patches illustrated, mainly pocket patches, are those of armored cavalry regiments (A.C.R.) and some were also worn during World War 2. Some modified patches of the 1st Cavalry Division were used by the divisional artillery; the 'Medevac' patch was worn, numbered, by only twenty-six helicopter pilots, usually on the left pocket, on the right if the wearer had been previously shot down.

The patch of the 163rd A.C.R. is similar to that of the 163rd R.C.T. because they are technically one unit. It was raised in 1884–7 as the 1st Infantry Regiment of the Montana N.G.; redesignated 163rd Infantry Regiment in 1922, it was inducted into Federal service in 1940 as part of the 41st Infantry Division. After the War it became the infantry regiment of the 163rd R.C.T. and in 1953 an armoured cavalry regiment.

Plate 41. Shoulder Sleeve and Pocket Insignia
Armored Force

The tricoloured triangular insignia was adopted by the Armored Corps during World War 1; the colours, yellow, blue and red, are those of the cavalry, infantry and artillery, which are the basic components of the armoured formations.

The lightning, tank tracks and cannon, on round patches in branch-of-service colours, were the insignia of the 7th Mechanised Cavalry Brigade, formed in 1937 and composed of the 1st and 13th (Mech.) Cavalry Regiments, 68th F.A. Regiment, 47th Engineers Squadron and service units.

The Armored Force was formed on 10 July 1940 and its insignia, authorised on 7 May 1941, was the triangular patch of the former Armored Corps with the insignia of the 7th Mechanised Cavalry Brigade in its centre.

Roman numerals in the yellow apex of the shoulder patch distinguished the Armored Corps: these patches have been made with numbers from I to V and XVIII, although such corps never existed. The I Corps was disbanded in 1943, after the invasion of Sicily and the II, III and IV Corps became the 18th, 19th and 20th Army Corps respectively, with different patches altogether. The V Corps was never formed.

During World War 2, divisional patches were made numbered from 1 to 22, although only the divisions 1 to 14, 16 and 20 actually existed. The divisions numbered 27, 30, 40, 48, 49 and 50 belong to the National Guard. Many shoulder patches have straight tabs at the bottom, with black or dark blue lettering on yellow background. Also khaki tabs with yellow lettering have been used.

The following are the divisional titles embroidered on the tabs:

'OLD IRONSIDES'	1st Armored Division
'HELL ON WHEELS'	2nd Armored Division
'SPEARHEAD'	3rd Armored Division
'BREAKTHROUGH'	4th Armored Division
'VICTORY'	5th Armored Division
'SUPER SIXTH'	6th Armored Division
'LUCKY SEVENTH'	7th Armored Division
'IRON DUCE' 'IRON SNAKE' 'THUNDERING HERD' }	8th Armored Division
'PHANTOM' 'REMAGEN' }	9th Armoured Division
'TIGER'	10th Armored Division
'THUNDERBOLT'	11th Armored Division
'HELLCAT' 'SPEED IS THE PASSWORD' }	12th Armored Division
'BLACK CAT'	13th Armored Division
'LIBERATOR'	14th Armored Division
'EMPIRE'	27th Armored Division
'VOLUNTEERS' 'DIXIE' }	30th Armored Division
'GRIZZLY'	40th Armored Division
'HURRICANE'	48th Armored Division
'LONE STAR'	49th Armored Division
'JERSEY BLUES'	50th Armored Division

More than 200 shoulder patches of armoured battalions exist as well, with numbers running from 41 to well over 800. Some have additional tabs, for instance:

'BATTLEAXE'	526th Armored Battalion
'FLAME THROWER'	713th Armored Battalion
'DAREDEVILS'	740th Armored Battalion
'LITTLE DIVISION'	771st Armored Battalion

Shoulder patches with red numerals are worn by units of Armored engineers or artillery. A few regimental patches exist as well, as in the case of that of the 1st Bn/151st Armor, a unit of the Alabama N.G.

Personnel serving at the U.S. Army General Headquarters have 'GHQ' embroidered on the yellow apex of their insignia, while personnel of the Headquarters Armored Force have the letters 'HQ' only. The personnel of some other major organisations wear tabs below the patch, instead of letters on the patch, for instance, 'USATC ARMOR', 'USA ARMOR CENTER', 'THE ARMORED CENTER', 'THE ARMORED SCHOOL', 'THE ARMOR SCHOOL' and 'HONOR GUARD'.

The 112th Armored Cavalry Regiment wears the tank insignia with its regimental title on the tab, as a pocket patch, while the 5th and 7th Armored Cavalry Regiments have the regimental number and abbreviation 'CAV' embroidered on the patch, the latter in yellow.

The following letters can also be found embroidered on the shoulder patches: 'S' (School), 'DR' (Demonstration Regiment), 'RCN' (Reconnaissance). The latter title can also be shown by a 'RECON' tab. All personnel of the 7th Army Tank Training Center have the letters 'TTC' on the yellow apex of their patches and '17/GP' stands for 17th Armored Group.

The Airborne tab above the triangular patch was worn by a special unit just before the invasion of Japan.

A great number of pocket patches are worn by personnel of the various tank battalions and armoured cavalry regiments (Plate 40) of the armoured divisions. A yearly tank qualification course is held at Grafenwöhr, Germany, and a badge is issued afterwards with the year of the course at the bottom and often with 'DISTINGUISHED CREW' embroidered at the top. Illustrated below is the patch of the 14th Armored Cavalry Regiment which belongs to the same course.

Plate 42. Shoulder Sleeve and Pocket Insignia
Para. Glider, Abn Infantry, Glider Infantry and Para.
Infantry Regiments

The titles of the regiments of the Airborne divisions are related to their roles: thus they are known as Airborne Infantry (A.I.R.), Parachute Infantry (P.I.R.), Glider Infantry (G.I.R.) or Parachute Glider Infantry regiments (P.G.I.).

During World War 2, and since then, many regiments have changed their roles, some have been disbanded or absorbed by others, and most have worn more than one insignia. The 187th, 188th, 503rd and 511th were regiments of the 11th Airborne Division and battalions of the 187th, 188th and 511th were later part of 11th Air Assault Division (Test) which subsequently became the 1st Air Cavalry Division.

The 503rd P.I.R. was dropped in 1945 on the narrow highland on the western side of the fortress island of Corregidor. The dropping zone was very narrow and windswept and therefore the troop carriers flew in a single line and only six men could be dropped on each pass. After the war the 503rd adopted a new patch to commemorate the assault on the Rock of Corregidor.

The regiments of the 11th Airborne Division have also worn patches similar to the divisional one, but with the regimental number instead of the divisional number in the centre. The Division occupied Japan, so the 511th A.I.R. wore a patch with a Torii gate in its centre. The 187th Regiment also took part in the Korean War.

The 327th, 501st, 502nd and 506th were regiments of the 101st Airborne Division; the 325th, 504th and 505th belonged to the 82nd Airborne Division. During the North African/Mediterranean campaign part of the 509th P.I.R. was attached to the latter division and later, in North Western Europe, some other regiments (502nd, 506th, 507th, 508th and 517th) became provisionally part of the 82nd Airborne Division.

There are variations of the smaller patch of the 504th P.I.R. with company letters ('A', 'B', 'C', 'D', 'E', 'F', 'G', 'H', 'I', 'K', 'L', 'M', 'H and J HQ') on the shield and also a regimental patch of German manufacture. The third patch on the right was worn in the Lebanon in 1958.

The 509th was an Independent Parachute regiment. Some of its personnel wore the shoulder patch of the 5th Army below a scroll with the title 'PARACHUTE' during World War 2. A variation of the pocket patch of the reconnaissance platoon of the 509th has the figures '2/509' embroidered at the bottom.

Large cloth replicas of the distinctive insignia (D.I.) have been used as pocket patches by most regiments. I have illustrated only some examples of these as the D.I., and not the patch, is the original badge.

Plate 43. Shoulder Sleeve and Pocket Insignia
Airborne and Parachute Infantry Regts and Miscellaneous Para. Units

The 13th Airborne Division was formed by the 189th and 190th G.I.R. and by the 513th P.I.R. and, eventually, the two Glider Infantry regiments became the 326th G.I.R. The 513th P.I.R. was transferred to 17th Airborne Division, replaced in the 13th by the 515th P.I.R. The Division arrived in Europe in 1945 but only its 517th Combat Team saw combat action.

The 17th Airborne Division consisted of the 193rd and 194th G.I.R.; the 507th (Plate 42) and, since March 1944, the 513th P.I.R. also joined its numbers. The 550th Airborne Infantry Bn was attached to the Division during the Battle of the Ardennes and the Crossing of the Rhine.

Patches of the 542nd P.I.R. exist on blue or on grey background and there is a patch of the 550th P.I.R. with the motto 'A BOLT FROM THE BLUE' embroidered on a scroll below the shield.

The parachute field artillery battalions and the airborne engineers were part of the divisions: some other patches, mainly D.I. replicas, exist as well.

The green Aerial Supply badge was worn by the airborne detachment of U.S. TASCOM, Europe. A pocket patch of the Golden Knights, with the knight's helmet, has no 'AIRBORNE' designation above the parachute.

Plate 44. Shoulder Sleeve and Pocket Insignia
Airborne Divisions, Brigades and Other Units

In 1946 the former 80th, 84th and 100th Infantry Divisions were reactivated as airborne divisions of the Organised Reserve, as well as the 108th, a new division with a new shoulder patch. They became infantry divisions in 1952.

The 1st Battalion of the 225th Infantry Regiment wore the patch of the 46th N.G. Division (Plate 35) with an 'AIRBORNE' tab.

The 6th, 9th, 18th, 21st and 135th are known as 'ghost airborne divisions' because, although a great number of their patches have been made, the divisions have never existed (see also Plate 35).

A miscellany of patches has been illustrated under the heading of Airborne Brigades and Other Units, starting with the shoulder patch of the 2nd Airborne Brigade, worn during World War 2. The two pocket patches of the 173rd Airborne Brigade have been worn unofficially in Vietnam and the fourth is the pocket patch worn by personnel of an airborne unit of the 24th Infantry Division. The patch of the 24th, with an 'AIRBORNE' tab, has been used by the 187th (1st Brigade) and by the 503rd Airborne Infantry Regiment, in several variations, with attached and detached tabs. The 509th A.I.R. wore the patch of the 8th Infantry Division as well, with an 'AIRBORNE' tab attached.

The airborne patch of the 2nd Field Force was worn by personnel of 'D' Company, 75th Infantry Regiment.

A selection of shoulder sleeve and pocket insignia of units of the 82nd and 101st Airborne Divisions are illustrated in this plate. Both Divisions have coloured and subdued patches and the 101st has two versions of the latter, the first with 'AIRBORNE' and the eagle's head in black on an olive-green background and the other in reversed colours. Some coloured and subdued patches of the 101st have 'VIETNAM' on the tab and subdued patches exist with the eagle facing left or right and with the following abbreviations on the tab: '327th INF', '501st INF', '502nd INF', '506th INF', '787th INF', '320th ARTY', '326th ENGR', '101st AVN BN', '101st MP CO', '101st QM CO', '801st MAINT' and 'ABN SPT CMD'.

The patch of the 7th Ranger Bn was worn during the Korean War.

Italy

King Victor Emmanuel II was the creator of the Italian nation. When, in 1849, he succeeded to the throne as King of Sardinia (and Piedmont), the Italian peninsula was still divided into several independent states, which were slowly annexed to Piedmont until finally, in 1861, the Kingdom of Sardinia became the Kingdom of Italy.

After the Wars of Independence came the period of the Wars of Expansion, by which the Italians struggled to conquer an empire of their own. Italy was, however, a poor nation, dependent in many ways on the good will of the great powers, and the time came when the Italian leaders and the people did not know whether they were fighting for independence, expansion or survival. By 1943 Italy had collapsed, the country had become a battlefield, and Italian soldiers wore foreign uniforms. No national traditions seemed to be left.

The Italian soldiers who, in the van of the Allied armies, finally occupied Northern Italy wore British uniforms with Italian badges. The cap badges and collar patches remained those they wore before 1943 and, after the War, many officers were still wearing the old grey-green uniforms. The first Italian-made uniforms were very similar to the British battledress but without patch pockets on the trousers; the khaki blouse had two patch pockets with rectangular flaps. Summer uniforms were made of a greenish-yellow material and were composed of shirt and tie, and trousers. The forage cap was standard army head-dress but personnel of the armoured units wore a black beret.

Soon after the war a new khaki uniform was introduced for the officers, warrant officers and N.C.O.s and it is still issued today in winter and summer versions. It is composed of a peaked cap and a single-breasted jacket with open collar and four patch pockets with rectangular flaps; all buttons are gilded and bear the arm-of-service badge. This jacket is always worn with a belt of matching material and the trousers are also made of the same material.

The greatcoat is also made of khaki material; it is double-breasted, with side pockets and shoulder straps. The same pattern of greatcoat is worn by all ranks, although that of the soldiers is made of a coarser material and is fastened with plastic buttons, whilst the officers, warrant officers and N.C.O.s' greatcoat has gilded buttons.

Several other utility garments have been adopted since 1945, for instance the sleeveless leather jacket of the tank troops (used during the war by the British Army), camouflage overalls and olive-green jackets.

A new ceremonial uniform for officers was adopted in 1956. It is basically black, although a white jacket is prescribed for summer wear. A dark blue (infantry blue) greatcoat has to be worn with this uniform. The winter version consists of a black peaked cap and a black double-breasted jacket with open collar showing the white shirt and black tie. The trousers and shoes are also black. The lapels of the jacket are pointed and small rectangular ornamentations are worn in place of the shoulder straps on both the jacket and greatcoat.

All Bersaglieri still wear the wide-brimmed black hat with cockerel feathers when on parade or special duties; ordinarily they wear the red fez with blue tassel. Mountain troops usually wear their traditional feathered hat although several patterns of mountain field cap, with folding sides, have also been adopted in turn since the end of the War. In the 1950s the stiff kepi, now lined with khaki material, was reintroduced as parade head-dress of the horse artillery. The parachutists wore khaki berets until 1960; then they adopted grey-green berets and, finally, maroon berets in 1968. The British helmets worn during the latter stages of the war by the Royal Italian Army were soon replaced by Italian helmets whilst, by contrast, the webbing equipment of British pattern is still used nowadays.

Plate 45. Cap Insignia

In June 1946 Italy became a republic and therefore the Royal Crown and all the symbols of the House of Savoy were eliminated from all official Italian emblems. However, part of Italy had temporarily become a republic some years before and the same process had already taken place then. The crown was cut off the generals' cap badges in 1943 and the year after new badges were made without the Cross of Savoy. Thus, after 1946, entirely new cap badges were adopted for the generals. They represent the eagle superimposed on a wreath of laurel and oak leaves, with a shield charged with the letters 'R' and 'I' (Repubblica Italiana) interlaced on its breast. The generals' cap badges are usually embroidered in gold or silver wire on a red background but white and gilded metal cap badges can be found as well, without coloured backing. The Generals of Brigade and Division wear silver cap badges, the senior generals gold badges. All the officers, including generals, wear woven cap bands with oak leaf design on the peaked cap, while the other ranks wear a ribbon-type cap band. The chin strap has lost its original supporting role and it is now an ornament which shows the rank and class of rank of the wearer. The generals wear three silver twisted cords, the senior officers two gold twisted cords and the junior officers a stripe of gold lace. One, two or three narrow stripes of gold lace with black edges, all woven in one piece, show the rank. Two are worn, slipped one on each side of the chin strap. The warrant officers wear leather chin straps with one, two or three stripes of W.O.'s lace at the sides. All the other ranks wear plain leather chin straps. Illustrated in this plate are the chin straps of a General of Brigade, a Lieutenant-Colonel, a Captain and a Warrant Officer. The rank badges illustrated below the chin straps have been worn on a variety of head-dresses (khaki, black, grey-green and maroon berets, mountain field caps and forage caps) which I have loosely described as field caps, although they are not necessarily worn only with the field uniform. These badges used to be worn on the left side of the head-dress and were abolished in February 1971. The officers' rank was shown by gold-embroidered stars, the warrant officers' rank by stripes. The generals' stars were embroidered on silver lace, the senior officers wore stars surrounded by a rectangular gold frame (3 × 5–6 cm., depending on the number of stars) embroidered in gold on khaki, black, etc. material, matching the colour of the head-dress. The three stars of the Colonel Regimental Commander were edged in brick red. The stars of the junior officers were embroidered individually and then stitched on the cap. The Aiutante di Battaglia had three W.O.'s stripes on a red backing. The officers of the mountain troops wear gold lace stripes on the left side of the grey-green cap, behind the gilded feather holder. The centre of the officer's feather holder is usually blank but holders with the Cross of Savoy in its centre are still worn. The O.R.s' feather holder is an oval woollen pompom, of a different colour for each battalion. Enamel badges (Plate 50) are worn pinned on the left side of the cap.

Plate 46. Officers' and Warrant Officers' Rank Badges

In March 1945 the officers' rank badges were moved once again onto the shoulder straps, as they used to be worn before 1934. The generals wear from one to three gold stars on silver lace shoulder straps; Army Corps Generals with Special Appointments (i.e. Army Chief of Staff, Defence Chief of Staff) wear another gold star but with red edging. The same generals wear a fourth stripe with red edging also on the sides of the chin strap.

The senior officers wear gold stars with a stripe of gold lace around the loose ends of the shoulder straps and junior officers wear the stars only. The warrant officers already wore their own gold and black stripes on the shoulder straps, those of the Aiutante di Battaglia being on a red background.

Plate 47. Officers' Rank Badges (Black Uniform)

When the black uniform was first adopted the rank badges were worn on the shoulders of the jacket and greatcoat, and small gilded arm-of-service badges (miniature replicas of the cap badges) were worn on the lapels of the jacket, below the national stars. The rank badges were rectangular (about 3 × 6 cm.) and the stars and frames embroidered on black or white background, depending on whether they had to be worn on black or on white jackets. The generals' badges had a silver background.

In 1963 all the badges of the black uniform were modified. Sleeve rank badges, similar to those worn from 1934 to 1945, were readopted and the arm-of-service badges were moved onto the shoulder frames where the rank stars were previously. Thus the generals now wear small embroidered eagles in the frames and the traditional *greca* and stripes on the sleeves. The stripes are commonly called *lasagne* and the Army Corps General with Special Appointment wears four, the top horizontal stripe edged in red. The senior officers wear a large (1·5-cm.-wide) stripe and from one to three narrow (6-mm.-wide) ones, the regimental commanders on a brick red background. The junior officers wear from one to three narrow stripes.

Sergeants and Corporals

The sergeants of the Italian Army wear V-shaped gold chevrons formed by a large stripe and one or two smaller ones, which are woven in one piece and then stitched into shape on khaki cloth.

The corporals wear black chevrons, except for those of the Parachute Brigade who wear red chevrons on sky blue cloth.

The chevrons are usually worn on both upper sleeves, below the formation sign, if any is worn. On the camouflage overalls and olive-green field jackets only one chevron is worn, stitched above the left pocket. Only one chevron is worn with the summer uniform, stitched below the formation sign onto a 'tongue' hanging from the shirt's left shoulder strap.

Cadets

The three badges illustrated at the bottom of this plate are made of metal and are sewn on slip-ons worn on the shoulder straps of the summer shirts. The letters 'AUC' stand for Allievo Ufficiale di Complemento and are worn by conscripted officer cadets. The N.C.O. cadets wear the letters 'AS', standing for Allievo Sottufficiale, and the cadet squad leaders wear the letters 'ACS' – Allievo Comandante di Squadra.

Gold or silver stripes of lace on the collar of the jacket, blouse or greatcoat replace the badges on the winter uniforms. The gold stripe of the A.U.C. and A.S. is stitched along the edges of the collar, all around, starting from below the collar patches if they are worn. The silver stripe of the A.C.S. is worn only at the front, from below the collar patches to the level of the shoulder straps.

Cap Badges

Until 1946 the army was officially known as the Regio Esercito, or Royal Army, and when Italy became a republic the title was changed to Esercito

Italiano, Italian Army. During 1945 and 1946 three types of cap badges were made on a khaki background: large badges, embroidered in gold wire, worn on the peaked cap by officers, warrant officers and sergeants; small gold-embroidered badges for field caps; and the black machine-embroidered badges for corporals and soldiers. Previously they had worn their old badges embroidered on grey-green on the khaki uniform. In 1946 all crowns and royal emblems were abolished; thus the Infantry and the Lancers had their crown replaced by flames; but most army services (Medical, Administrative, etc.) replaced the Royal Crown with the new Crown of the Republic. Cap badges which had no royal emblems (Bersaglieri, mountain troops, Grenadiers, Dragoons, Artillery, Engineers, etc.) remained the same. Since 1945 some of the badges illustrated in these plates have been abolished and others have been adopted in the meantime.

The officers, warrant officers and sergeants wear hand-embroidered badges; large ones embroidered on khaki, black and brick red are found on the peaked cap, and smaller ones on the field cap. Also plastic imitations of gold-embroidered cap badges are used at present and will eventually replace the hand-made ones.

In the last twenty-eight years corporals and soldiers have worn several different types of cap badge, ranging from small brass badges and machine-embroidered badges to plastic and white metal badges. On 15 February 1971 new regulations were published which prescribe the last type, still in use at present.

Plate 48. Cap Badges

A selection of different cap badges is illustrated here: the gold hand-embroidered badges of Infantry, Bersaglieri, Grenadiers, Lancers and some of the badges of the Artillery and Engineers.

The infantry, artillery and engineers of the Folgore Infantry Division wear special cap badges granted to commemorate the exploits of the old Folgore Division at the Battle of Alamein. The infantrymen wear the old divisional cap badge but without the Royal Crown. Artillery men wear Field Artillery cap badges superimposed on crossed swords. The divisional engineers wear the badge of the Pionieri d'Arresto (Plate 49). The khaki beret is the divisional head-dress.

The Lagunari are the amphibious troops of the army. They were formed in 1951 and are stationed and trained on the lagoons of the Northern Adriatic. All ranks wear black berets with gold or yellow thread embroidered cap badges.

The white metal parachutists' badge illustrated is currently worn on the maroon beret by all ranks of the Parachute Brigade. Previously a bi-metal badge was worn by the other ranks on the grey-green beret, whilst the officers, W.O.s and N.C.O.s had gold and silver hand-embroidered badges which, previously, were also embroidered on khaki, for wear on the khaki beret. A new badge for all the Armoured Cavalry was adopted in 1971 and another of these newly-adopted white metal badges is that of the A.A. Artillery. A roundel with the regimental number is fixed onto the centre of the badges. The Dragoons and Engineers' cap badges shown respectively in the 2nd and last row were used soon after the War. They were made of brass and had some small holes for stitching them on the head-dress. Later the O.R.s' cap badges were machine-embroidered in yellow thread on a black background for all armoured units (see Armoured Artillery) and in black thread on khaki for the rest of the army (Plate 49, Medical Service). Subsequently other badges were made in yellow or gold plastic (see Territorial Air Defence) and black plastic (Plate 49, Clerks and Supply Service).

The tank troops for a time wore a brass badge which in the 1930s used to be worn by officers on metal shoulder boards. The badge of the 1930s, however, used to be gilded.

The Heavy A.A. Artillery and the Light A.A. Artillery have been amalgamated and now wear the cap badge of the latter.

Plate 49. Cap Badges

The branch of the Engineers now known as Pionieri d'Arresto wear a special cap badge which is a combination of the Engineers' cap badge and the arm badge of the Guastatori (Plate 54).

Until 1946 a cog-wheel used to be in the centre of the Motor Transport's badge with the Savoy Knot just below. In 1946 the knot was abolished and the cog-wheel became a steering wheel.

The cap badge marked as N.B.C. is worn by personnel of the Nuclear, Biological and Chemical Defence units and, together with that of the Military Postal Service, was adopted in 1971.

The kepi badge worn by the cadets of the Modena Academy is illustrated in the bottom row. It is always superimposed on the national cockade.

Plate 50. Mountain Troops' Cap Badges

The mountain troops still wear their own traditional cap badges on all forms of head-dress. The Mountain Infantry (Alpini) cap badge shows an eagle clutching a bugle, superimposed on crossed rifles; the Mountain Artillery's badge has the eagle and bugle above crossed cannons, and the Engineers and Signals, the eagle and bugle above crossed axes. The latter has electric sparks added all around the axes. There are badges of the Motor Transport with and without the bugle and in all other cases the eagle is depicted just above the arm-of-service badges. The officers, warrant officers and N.C.O.s wear badges embroidered in gold on grey-green felt for the traditional grey-green hat, embroidered in gold on khaki for the khaki peaked cap and on black felt for the black peaked cap. There also exist some small gold-embroidered cap badges for the khaki mountain field cap. The Alpini wear machine-embroidered or black plastic cap badges with a green centre on the grey-green hat. The cadets at the Mountain School wear gold plastic badges. They wear smaller gold or black plastic badges and badges embroidered in black thread on khaki on the mountain field cap. The regimental commanders wear large gold eagles embroidered on brick red felt. The generals of the Mountain Medical Service have the gold eagle embroidered on amaranth felt.

Enamel Badges

All ranks of the mountain troops wear enamel badges on the grey-green hat, near the feather holder. Initially there was one badge for each alpine battalion and mountain artillery group, but a great number of badges have been made in recent years to commemorate the brigades, the regiments, the companies and various support services of each brigade. These badges are usually self-explanatory, depicting regimental and company numbers, feathers and coloured feather holders, local mountains, mottoes, etc. For instance, the badge of the Agordo Group shows its regimental number (it is the 6th Mountain Artillery Regiment) and demonstrates that the group is formed by the 41st, 42nd and 43rd Batteries. The coat of arms of Agordo is shown and the regimental motto, in the local dialect, reads 'Men, rocks and guns, all one piece.'

Some other army units have adopted enamel badges which are usually worn pinned on one of the breast pockets. Illustrated on the left is a badge of the Territorial Air Defence and one of a unit of self-propelled guns.

Collar Patches

These patches are worn on the collar of jackets, blouses and shirts and for a time some larger ones were also worn on the collar of the greatcoat. Smaller patches, usually made of plastic or metal and enamel are used for summer uniforms, on the shirt collar. The Infantry regimental patches are made of felt and Russia braid, or are woven or made of printed ribbon. After the war patches were made of metal, painted in regimental colours, and later, for almost two decades, they were made of plastic. A number of different types of plastic were used and the badges were also made in different sizes. Some recent regulations, however, have introduced a new standard type of collar patch made of metal and coloured enamels. Technically the collar patches are of rectangular shape and in Italy are known as *mostrine*. The collar patches of the Grenadiers, also rectangular, are, however, called *alamari*. The pointed patches are known as 'flames'.

Plate 51. Collar Patches

The Infantry collar patches were adopted in 1902 and at that time were much longer than the present patches; they used to have pointed ends and a small silver button on one side, and a star on the other side, at the front. Plain rectangular collar patches were adopted in 1934 and are still in use at present. After 1946 the Re (King) Brigade, with the black patch with two red stripes, was re-titled Piemonte, and the Regina (Queen) Brigade, with white collar patch, became the Bari Brigade. A great number of Infantry regiments have been formed and subsequently disbanded in the last twenty-eight years and due to the fact that a modern division is composed of three Infantry regiments, the brigade system has ceased to exist. The complete range of the Infantry collar patches can only be illustrated in a volume dealing with World War 1, as most regiments were disbanded in 1919 and never raised again.

All the Cavalry flames which have existed since 1945, have been illustrated. The first four regiments were Dragoons, the 5th, 6th, 7th and 8th regiment were Lancers, the 19th used to be a regiment of Guides and all the others Light Cavalry. The 3rd Savoia Cavalry Regiment was renamed Gorizia and later it became Savoia again, but the collar patch was slightly changed. The Cavalry flames and all the other two- or one-pointed flames are made of coloured felts, plastic or metal and enamel. The Signals, which used to be part of the Engineers, became an independent branch of the army in 1955. All ranks of the Armoured Infantry wear a small brass tank in the centre of their Infantry cap badge, in place of the regimental numbers.

Plate 52. Collar Patches

The Artillery, Engineers and all the services of the alpine brigades and armoured troops wear their original collar patches, superimposed on a rectangular green or blue background respectively. There is no Veterinaries patch with blue background for the armoured troops.

The parachutists of the Parachute Brigade wear special collar patches: the winged sword and parachute could be found embroidered in gold and silver on the patch or, made of metal, can be pinned onto the patch. Some years ago members of the Parachute platoon of the alpine brigades used to wear the green flames on the para. patches, but without parachute. They also used to wear a special enamel badge. Personnel of the Folgore Infantry Division wear similar collar patches, also without the parachute. All the personnel of both the Parachute Brigade and Folgore Infantry Division, except infantrymen, wear their special patches on the blue patch, below the star. Infantrymen of the 183rd Infantry Regiment of the Folgore Division wore plain collar patches whilst infantrymen of the 53rd and 82nd regiments of the same division now wear a small regimental patch below the winged sword; the first, green with a white stripe, and the second, blue with a yellow stripe.

There is only one cap badge for all the Technical Services (Plate 49), while the collar patches are black with piping in the colour of the arm of service, as follows:

yellow	Artillery Service
crimson	Engineers Service
red	Chemical Service
green	Geographical Service
light blue	Signals Service
blue	Motor Transport Service

Plate 53. Miscellaneous Insignia

Until 1964 all qualified parachutists wore an embroidered or brass parachute on the left upper sleeve; the background of this badge was usually sky blue, but the Alpini parachutists wore it with a green background. A new badge was adopted in 1964 to be worn above the right breast pocket and was in gilded metal for officers and silver or white for the other ranks. The badge with the star is worn by the parachutists of the Parachute Brigade and the other, without star, by qualified army parachutists not belonging to that brigade.

The Military Parachute Centre, formed on 18 January 1947, was the first military parachute establishment. All its members wore a special badge made of metal and enamel. The badges for Riggers and Parachute Saboteurs are made of brass and enamel, the breast wings of the 1st Tactical Group are made of bronze and all the other badges are embroidered on the uniform material except for the badge of the Parachute Artillery which is embroidered on sky blue cloth.

The officers, warrant officers and sergeants of the Lagunari wear patches on the collar of their winter jackets, whilst the other ranks wear smaller patches on the cuffs. When in summer uniform, all ranks wear a badge on the breast of the shirt. These latter badges are made in brass and enamel or in brass, with the background painted red. Patches and badges show the winged Lion of St Mark on crossed rifles and an anchor. The collar patches are embroidered in gold, whilst the cuff patches are embroidered in yellow thread or made of plastic.

Plate 54. Specialists' Badges

Only a small selection of specialists' badges have been illustrated in this plate as a great number of such badges have been adopted since 1945.

Most are unofficial, some have been abolished and others have been changed. There are three types of specialists' badges, made of metal or plastic or embroidered.

Amongst the tank badges illustrated the only official one is the brass breast badge surrounded by the wreath and motto, worn by officers in brass or gilded brass, and in silver or white metal by the other ranks. The tank and dragon badge is also made in two variations, of brass and of white metal, and it is often worn, although unofficially. The Anti-Tank badge is made of brass and coloured enamels. The plastic arm badges for tank and armoured car crews are also unofficial; like the others they are made of plastic stamped onto khaki material. There also exists another triangular badge with the title 'Istruttore Milit. di Sci. e Alpinismo', with two skis in the centre as well. Motor-car and motorcycle drivers wear gold-embroidered arm badges as well; the small brass motor-car illustrated was worn until the 1950s, and other badges, embroidered in red thread, used to be worn during the War. That car was older in style and another one, older still, was worn in the early 1930s, embroidered in yellow. A vintage car, embroidered in wool, was worn on the arm during World War 1.

Specialists' Arm Shields and Pocket Badges

A great number of different specialists' arm shields have been worn since the end of the War. The tank crews wear four similar shields on which only the appointment title of the wearer is different, i.e. Tank Chief, Driver, Signaller and Gunner. The size of these shields is 5 × 6 cm. Some smaller shields have been made in recent years in two versions: one made of brass and enamel and the other made of brass and coloured plastic.

Plate 55. Arm Shields.
Infantry and Armoured Divisions and Brigades, Mountain Brigades and Miscellanea

The Italians call their formation signs *scudetti*, i.e. small shields, and they wear them stitched on the left upper sleeve or, with summer uniform, on a cloth tongue suspended from the shoulder strap.

After World War 2 Italy had five Combat Groups and three formations called Internal Security Divisions; the former eventually became infantry divisions and the latter infantry brigades.

Originally there were six Combat Groups: Folgore, Cremona, Legnano, Friuli, Mantova and Piceno, but the last became a training unit in January 1945.

Later another infantry division was formed, the Granatieri di Sardegna, stationed in Rome and composed of Grenadiers and the 17th Infantry

Regiment. The Aosta, Avellino, Pinerolo and Trieste are independent infantry brigades.

The Ariete and Centauro are armoured divisions, formed by tank and armoured cavalry regiments, while the Pozzuolo del Friuli Armoured Brigade is formed by regiments of armoured cavalry only. The Italian units stationed in Somaliland (Corpo di Sicurezza della Somalia), before this former colony became independent, wore a special blue and red shield with a leopard in its centre.

The five alpine brigades wear shields with the brigade emblem on a green background, which is the colour of the mountain troops.

The Folgore Parachute Brigade consists of the brigade headquarters, the 1st Parachute Regiment, units of airborne artillery and engineers, and support services. The 1st Parachute Regiment was formed in 1962 and the year after all parachute units were formed into a brigade. A yellow thunderbolt (*folgore*) was added some years later to the original arm shield. The 1st Tactical Group is the spearhead of the Brigade. The 3rd Missile Brigade also has an independent unit of parachutists, the Gruppo Acquisizione Obiettivi (Acquisition–Objective Group). These men are initially trained by the Italian Parachute School and subsequently they undertake further training with the U.S. forces of SETAF. Therefore they wear the U.S. Parachute badge as well.

All troops of the garrison in Trieste wear a special badge which depicts the white halberd, taken from the town's coat of arms, on a shield divided into the national colours.

In the late 1940s the officers, warrant officers and sergeants used to wear hand-embroidered shields and the corporals and soldiers used to wear woven ones. Later, woven badges were replaced by plastic badges. Some shields have also been made of metal, usually brass, with painted background.

Plate 56. Training Schools' Arm Shields

These come in three variations: hand-embroidered, woven and plastic, although some O.R.s' shields exist only in two variations, woven or made of plastic. For instance, the first O.R.s' pattern of the Armoured Troops School badge was woven whilst the second pattern was only made in plastic. There is also a similar badge for mechanised troops with 'SC. TR. MECCANIZZATE' written above the shield. These arm shields are mostly self-explanatory.

Germany

Before and during World War 2 Germany expanded territorially in Central Europe but by the spring of 1945 it was completely overrun by the Allied armies which, after the German surrender, assumed supreme authority. It was divided into zones of occupation administered by British, American, Russian and French Military Governors. The capital city of Berlin, in the heart of the Russian Zone, was similarly divided among the victors.

They also formed a Control Council for the administration of Germany as a whole, but the Russians withdrew from it in March 1948.

Since the Fusion Agreement signed in December 1946 the British and U.S. Zones, and later the French Zone, joined in an economic union and subsequently a Parliamentary Council elected by the Diets of the western zones drafted a provisional constitution. The first Federal Government came to office after the publication of the Basic Law, in 1949.

In the zone occupied by the Soviet Army, the People's Council, appointed in 1948, became the People's Chamber, which approved the first Constitution in 1949. The German Democratic Republic was founded on 7 October 1949.

Meanwhile, in Western Germany, when the Federal Government took office, the Allied Military Governors became High Commissioners and when, in 1955, the Federal Republic of Germany became a sovereign nation, they became Ambassadors.

German Federal Republic

The armed forces of the Federal Republic are known as the Bundeswehr and were raised in accordance with the 1955 treaties which provided for Germany's military contribution to NATO.

The first dress regulations are dated 23 July 1955 and the first uniforms were shown to the public on 12 November 1955. The new uniforms adopted in 1955 had no connection whatsoever with the traditional German military dress: all ranks wore grey service and walking-out uniforms, olive-green fatigue uniforms and a camouflage battledress. The grey jackets were double-breasted with two rows of buttons and an open collar, showing the shirt and tie underneath. Officers and sergeants wore longer walking-out jackets than the other ranks, who had only one jacket, considerably shorter, which technically was the service dress jacket worn by all ranks.

The walking-out uniform consisted of the peaked cap, jacket, trousers and shoes. Officers wore white shirt and grey tie and the other ranks grey shirt and tie.

The 'mountain cap', with soft peak and folding sides, was worn with service dress, together with a cloth belt and boots with leggings, the latter subsequently being replaced by jackboots. The new steel helmet, on the American pattern, replaced the mountain cap on armed duties.

An olive-green mountain cap was worn with fatigue uniform, and the helmet with battledress. A grey winter greatcoat and a raincoat were also adopted in 1955 for all ranks' use and both are worn currently.

In January 1957 variations of traditional German collar patches replaced the metal collar badges previously worn and in the summer of the same year a new jacket was adopted for all ranks and is still in use nowadays. It is single-breasted with open collar, four metal buttons at the front and four patch pockets with flap and button. The grey of this jacket is a shade lighter than that of the trousers and head-dress. At the same time a black leather belt, with rectangular voided buckle, replaced the cloth belt previously worn with service dress. The pointed shoulder straps were changed back to the rounded shape in 1962 and during subsequent years other details of the uniform have been changed and new badges adopted. The peaked cap, which originally was round, has now resumed its original German shape and, in the meantime, the side cap has been readopted as well.

New uniforms were introduced for wear on special occasions and others to fit the needs of specialised warfare. The camouflage battledress was replaced by olive-green battledress, issued in summer and winter variations and considerably different for different branches of the army (i.e. airborne and mountain troops, and tank crews).

Plate 57. Cap Badges

The standard cap badge, worn by all ranks of the Bundeswehr, is the yellow, red and black national cockade which usually is worn above the crossed swords, the emblem of the army. When worn on the peaked cap, the crossed swords are superimposed on a wreath of oak leaves and they are worn on their own — below the cockade on all the other types of head-dress except the side cap, on which generally only the cockade is worn at the front. In certain cases, however, the swords are also worn on the side cap, above the cockade. They have to be bent in order to fit the top of the narrow front of the cap.

The peaked cap was introduced in 1955, to complement the walking-out dress and, at the same time, the grey and olive-green mountain caps were introduced respectively for service and fatigue uniforms. The generals wear gold-embroidered cap badges and the officers silver-embroidered cap badges on the peaked cap, both with embroidered cockades. The other ranks wear metal badges. The swords and oak wreath were of a yellow-brownish colour, known as 'old gold', until 1962 when new 'bright old gold' cap badges were issued to the other ranks. The peaked cap piping shows the class of rank of the wearer, i.e. gold piping for the generals and silver for the other officers. In 1955 the generals were granted a double row of gold-embroidered oak leaves on the visor of the peaked cap while all the others wore plain black visors until 1962, when one row of silver-embroidered oak leaves was granted to the senior officers and a silver ornament to the junior officers. The same ornament has also been worn by senior cadets (Oberfähnrich) since 1966.

Gold or silver piping is also worn on the grey mountain and side caps. A metal cockade and crossed swords are worn on the former and all mountain troops wear their traditional edelweiss as well, pinned on the left side. Olive-green and field-grey mountain caps are worn with the fatigue uniform and battledress respectively; their badges are coloured cockade and grey swords, machine-embroidered on one piece of material, the colour of which matches the uniform. The same composite badge was also worn until recently on the beret by tank troops who, together with reconnaissance troops, now wear a black beret with metal cap badge. Since 1971 all rifle units (Jäger) have been issued with green berets and airborne troops with Bordeaux-red berets, both with metal cap badges.

The side cap was originally adopted by the air force and later by the army. There are two army types, one made of grey cloth and worn with grey uniform and another, olive-green, worn by some units with battle-dress. A machine-embroidered cockade is worn on the latter.

Plate 58. Officers' Rank Badges (1955–62)

The standard jacket, adopted in 1955 by the Army of the Bundeswehr, had pointed shoulder straps on which the officers' rank was shown by an arrangement of stars and oak wreaths. The square-shaped stars were similar to those used until 1945 whilst the wreaths were new badges; adopted in order to distinguish the senior ranks.

The generals wore a piping of twisted gold cords around the loose sides of the shoulder straps, gold buttons, gold oak wreaths and stars. Initially there were only three generals' ranks. The rank of full General was created in 1956 and, as the standard stars (21 mm. in diameter) were too large, some new smaller stars (19 mm.) were made for this new rank.

The officers wore a silver cord piping around the shoulder straps with old gold buttons and old gold wreaths and stars. It should be noted that the first senior officers' wreaths were straight. On 1 February 1956 the officers' rank badges were changed to silver and rounded oak wreaths were adopted for the senior officers. In 1959 the buttons of the shoulder straps were also changed to silver.

Plate 59. N.C.O.s' Rank Badges (1955–7)

Three different types of N.C.O.s' rank badges were introduced in 1955: the four senior N.C.O.s wore their rank badges on the shoulder straps in the form of small old gold metal chevrons, in singles and doubles one above the other. The Stabsunteroffizier and Unteroffizier wore chevrons on the upper sleeves and the others wore stripes (half chevrons) on the upper sleeves. These chevrons were made of old gold lace (10 mm. wide) and were woven in a single stripe or in two and three stripes with a dark grey line in between.

1957–9

On 26 July 1957 the new rank of Hauptfeldwebel was created and a new rank badge devised for senior N.C.O.s. It was a diamond-shaped loop made of metal with a brownish old gold finish. The small metal chevrons and the lace chevrons and stripes remained unchanged.

Plate 60. Officers' Rank Badges (1962)

In 1962, new shoulder straps with rounded ends were adopted by all ranks, with gold and silver piping for generals and officers respectively. Piping in arm-of-service colour was added in the form of a cloth underlay protruding all around the shoulder strap. However, many officers for a time wore the old pointed shoulder straps to which they had added the coloured underlay.

The standard old gold buttons were changed in 1959 to gold for generals, silver for officers and grey metal buttons for the other ranks. Later, in 1962, new wreaths and stars were adopted as well. They were both made of a lighter metal and the wreaths were narrower and the stars considerably smaller.

Plate 61. N.C.O.s' Rank Badges (1962–4 pattern)

Between 1957 and 1962 a new regulation, dated 8 June 1959, modified the N.C.O.s' rank badges. The N.C.O.s from Oberstabsfeldwebel to Unteroffizier, were now ordered to wear an old gold stripe around the loose sides of their shoulder straps. The individual rank badges, worn on the shoulder straps or on the sleeves, remained the same.

In 1962 the new rounded shoulder straps with coloured piping were adopted and the N.C.O.s' rank badges were also changed by the 12 November 1962 regulations. The Stabsunteroffizier and Unteroffizier's chevrons were abolished and all the N.C.O.s from Oberstabsfeldwebel to Stabsunteroffizier were entitled to the lace stripe all around the shoulder straps, while the Unteroffizier retained the stripe only around the loose ends of the straps. Thus the wearing of chevrons became unnecessary.

In practice the N.C.O.s, now entitled to the stripe all around the shoulder straps, added the short missing segment of lace on the old pointed shoulder straps, which were kept for a time until they wore out and new ones were made.

In 1964 the old gold badges and stripes were discarded. The new N.C.O.s' badges, still used nowadays, were similar in shape to the former types but made of oxidised white metal (technically called 'old silver') and in relief, whilst the former badges were flat. The stripes are narrower, only 8 mm. wide, made of greyish-yellow lace (bright old gold). The design of the lace has also changed. On 14 May 1973 the stripes on the sleeves were replaced by small old silver metal bars on the shoulder straps.

Plate 62. Officer Cadets' Rank Badges

The officer cadets wore a silver stripe slipped on the shoulder straps until 1962, when they adopted silver stars, worn on both forearms.

Since 1 February 1956 there have been two cadets' ranks: Fähnrich and Fahnenjunker, the former with a small metal chevron on the shoulder straps and the latter with one lace chevron on both upper sleeves.

The letters 'O A' stand for Offizieranwärter (officer candidate). They wore stripes on the upper sleeves.

The cadets' ranks went through stages of insignia changes just like those of other N.C.O.s. In 1959 both Fähnrich and Fahnenjunker adopted old gold stripes around the loose sides of their shoulder straps and, in 1962, the former started wearing the stripe all around the shoulder straps, whilst the Fahnenjunker lost the lace chevrons.

The rank of Oberfähnrich was instituted on 5 May 1966. Its insignia is the diamond-shaped loop, made of old silver, and worn on officers' shoulder straps.

Non-Commissioned Officer Cadets

Until 1 January 1973 the N.C.O. cadets wore a cuff title on both sleeves with the inscription 'Unteroffizierschule' followed by the Roman numerals I or II, embroidered in silver on a dark grey background. The cuff title is 30 mm. wide with silver edgings. Since 1958 the N.C.O. cadets have been appointed to corporal ranks after school training and their appointment is shown by a 6-cm. horizontal stripe above the usual corporal's stripes.

The letters 'UA' stand for Unteroffizieranwärter (N.C.O. candidate). On 14 May 1973 the stripes of the Gefreiter UA were replaced by small bars made of metal, worn on the shoulder straps.

Field Uniform Rank Badges

The generals, officers and sergeants wear different rank badges on field and fatigue uniforms whilst the corporals wear their usual stripes. The badges (wreaths, stars, etc.) are machine-embroidered on ready-made patches which are worn slipped on the shoulder straps or, in the case of uniforms without shoulder straps, stitched on the upper sleeves, below the national colours. The generals' rank badges are embroidered in yellow thread. As no arm-of-service badges are worn on field uniforms, since autumn 1962 a coloured band has often been worn slipped on at the end of the shoulder straps.

The national insignia is worn on both sleeves of the field uniform, at 6 cm. below the shoulder; it is a small machine-embroidered national flag, 5 × 2.5 cm. in size.

Plate 63. Collar Badges

In 1955 the new German Army was issued with metal collar badges, which were worn by all ranks on the collar of the grey jacket and of the fatigue uniform.

The generals wore their traditional gold-embroidered collar patches and officers of the General Staff Service also wore collar patches (Plate 64), whilst all the others wore metal badges. Personnel of the armoured units and of the Medical Service wore badges made in pairs, with the tanks and the snakes facing outward respectively; all the others were made in singles. Personnel of the Armoured Infantry should have worn a tank above crossed sabres and Reconnaissance Troops a shield superimposed on crossed lances, but due to the fact that metal badges were worn only for a short time the latter two badges were never used. The collar badges were made of solid metal with brownish old gold finish.

Miscellaneous Insignia

Before the adoption of divisional arm badges the mountain troops and the airborne troops wore distinguishing oval-shaped arm badges featuring an edelweiss and a parachute. The first one later became the divisional badge and the airborne troops adopted a parachute on a blue shield (Plate 66) as their divisional badge.

Qualified Mountain Guides wear their badge on the right breast pocket; it is very similar to that worn during the War but is now embroidered. The Hand-to-Hand Combat badge is also embroidered and worn on the right breast pocket.

The Marksman's lanyard was reintroduced in the early 1960s and it is worn attached to the right shoulder strap and to the first button of the jacket. The lanyard is made of twisted matt silver cords and is awarded in three classes, shown by a gold, silver or bronze badge pinned onto it at the shoulder.

The belt buckle is made of old silver metal and the same buckle is worn by all ranks, except generals who wear gold buckles.

Plate 64. Collar Patches

In 1955 only the generals and the officers of the General Staff Service wore collar patches. The first G.S. collar patches were embroidered on grey background cloth, later changed to the traditional crimson. On 1 January 1957 the traditional German double bars, embroidered on rectangular coloured patches, replaced the metal collar badges previously used. The arm-of-service colours adopted in 1957 were the following:

rifle-green	Infantry
grass-green	Armoured Infantry (Panzergrenadiere)
dark green	Anti-Tank Units
pink	Armoured Troops
golden-yellow	Armoured Reconnaissance
red	Artillery
coral-red	Army Anti-Aircraft
lemon-yellow	Signals
black	Engineers
Bordeaux-red	Atomic-Biological-Chemical Defence Troops

blue	Technical Troops
dark blue	Medical Troops
light blue	Quartermasters
orange	Military Police
light grey	Army Aviation
white	Military Bands

Subsequently, the collar patches of the Armoured Infantry, Anti-Tank units and Quartermasters were discarded and the first two became part of the Infantry, adopting its patches. The same green patches are also worn by rifle units, grenadiers, mountain and airborne troops. The remaining thirteen arm-of-service colours have also been shown on the shoulder straps since 1962, when piping was adopted.

The officers wear matt grey hand-embroidered collar patches, slightly longer than those of the other ranks, which are woven and measure 5.5 × 3 cm. in size.

Two O.R.s' collar patches have been illustrated in the bottom row of patches, at the left; the following three on the right are no longer in use, and like the others are now worn by officers.

Plate 65. Parachutists' Wings

The first type of parachute insignia (1) was adopted very early and vaguely resembles the wartime Close Combat clasp. It was worn above the right breast pocket of the jacket and it was made of old silver metal, although an embroidered type also existed for fatigue or field uniforms. Later, another breast badge was adopted (2), embroidered on grey felt in matt silver for officers and grey thread for other ranks. The third and final pattern (3) of parachutist's badge was adopted in 1965. It is a silver-embroidered badge and is issued in three classes, represented respectively by a gold, silver or bronze wreath. It is still worn above the right pocket.

Arm Badges

These arm badges are worn on the left forearm by specialised personnel and are usually hand-embroidered for officers and machine-embroidered for other ranks on a circular grey background. They were initially adopted by the Medical Service in four variations: for Doctors and medical personnel, Veterinaries, Pharmacists and Dentists. The generals of the Medical Service wore a badge embroidered in gold, officers wore silver-embroidered badges and the other ranks wore badges embroidered in grey thread. Veterinaries, Pharmacists and Dentists are always officers. By a new regulation of April 1972 Doctors, Veterinaries, Pharmacists and dental officers were granted new metal badges to be used on the shoulder straps instead of arm badges. The design of the badges remained unchanged, although the new badges are smaller and made of old silver for officers and gilded metal for generals. Some badges worn by the other ranks only show a letter of the alphabet, which stands for the wearer's qualifications, in the following order:

S	Schirrmeister	Storekeeper (vehicles, cars, etc.)
F	Feuerwerker	Artificer
I	Instandsetzungstruppführer	Repair Maintenance Fitter
W	Wallmeister	Fortification Maintenance
P	Prüfer	Equipment Inspector (Parachute units)
A	Absetzer	Rigger (Parachute units)

Cuff Titles

Another two cuff titles exist besides those of the N.C.O.s' schools. One is worn by the Guards Battalion stationed in Siegburg, near Bonn, and the other by all personnel of the Army Aviation. They are both 30 mm. wide, with silver edgings and lettering or wings hand- or machine-embroidered on a dark grey background.

Plate 66. Formation Badges

The formation badges were adopted in December 1962 and are still worn on the left upper sleeve by all ranks of the German Army.

The badges of the staff headquarters always have the German spread eagle in the centre; those of the training schools and depots have crossed swords in the centre while divisional badges show the emblem of the division.

The first badge illustrated is worn by personnel serving at the Ministry of Defence (*Bundesministerium der Verteidigung*) and it has a golden-yellow border with black lines. The same badge, but with a silver and black lined border, is worn by personnel of the Territorial Defence Command (*Kommando der Territorialen Verteidigung*); the personnel of the Bundeswehr's Central Military Stations (*Zentrale Militärische Bundeswehrdienststellen*) have a red border on the badge. The same badge, but with a dark blue border, is also worn at the Central Medical Stations (*Zentrale Sanitätsdienststellen*). Personnel of the six Military District Commands (*Wehrbereichskommandos* I–VI) wear the same badge with silver and black lined border and Roman numerals (from I to VI) below the eagle.

The third badge illustrated in this plate is that of the 1st Corps Headquarters. There are similar badges for the 2nd and 3rd Corps H.Q. The same badge with a pink border is worn by personnel of the 100th, 200th and 300th Tank Regiments, respectively part of the 1st, 2nd and 3rd Corps.

Personnel serving at depots wear crossed swords with a small flaming grenade beneath. The same badge, but with an 'L' or 'S' below the swords, are used by training and demonstration units. The badge with the 'L' is worn by soldiers serving in training brigades, or by demonstration units in training schools. The 'S' is worn by training staff, instructors and N.C.O. students. Identical badges, but with different borders, stand for different branches of training, as is explained below:

Border Colour	Branch of Training
silver/black stripes	Army Officers and N.C.O.s' Schools
	Heeresoffizierschulen
light grey	Army Aviation School
	Heeresfliegerwaffenschule
lemon-yellow	Signals School
	Fernmeldeschule
orange	Military Police School
	Feldjägerschule
rifle-green	Combat Schools I, III and IV (Infantry)
	Kampftruppenschulen I, III and IV
pink	Combat School II (Armour)
	Kampftruppenschule II
brick-red	Artillery School
	Artillerieschule
brick-red/blue stripes	Rocket School
	Raketenschule
green/white stripes	Airborne–Air Transportation School
	Luftlande–Lufttransportschule
coral-red	Anti-Aircraft School
	Flugabwehrschule
black	Engineers' School
	Pionierschule
Bordeaux-red	Atomic–Biological–Chemical Defence School
	A.B.C.–Abwehrschule
blue	School of Technical Troops
	Schule der Tech. Truppen I–III

The Army of the Bundeswehr has twelve divisions each with its divisional emblem on the badge. However, the personnel of the divisional headquarters of each division wear the badge with a silver border and black lines, those of the 1st brigade in each division, a plain white border, those of the 2nd brigade, a red border, and those of the 3rd, a yellow border. There are thus the following divisional-brigade badges:

Division	Brigade	Coloured Border
1st Armoured Division	H.Q.	silver/black lines
	1st Brigade	white
	2nd Brigade	red
	3rd Brigade	yellow
2nd Armoured Infantry Division (now Rifle Division)	H.Q.	silver/black lines
	4th Brigade	white
	5th Brigade	red
	6th Brigade	yellow
3rd Armoured Division	H.Q.	silver/black lines
	7th Brigade	white
	8th Brigade	red
	9th Brigade	yellow
4th Armoured Infantry Division (now Rifle Division)	H.Q.	silver/black stripes
	10th Brigade	white
	11th Brigade	red
	12th Brigade	yellow
5th Armoured Division	H.Q.	silver/black lines
	13th Brigade	white
	14th Brigade	red
	15th Brigade	yellow
6th Armoured Infantry Division	H.Q.	silver/black lines
	16th Brigade	white
	17th Brigade	red
	18th Brigade	yellow
7th Armoured Infantry Division	H.Q.	silver/black lines
	19th Brigade	white
	20th Brigade	red
	21st Brigade	yellow
1st Mountain Division	H.Q.	silver/black lines
	22nd Brigade	white
	23rd Brigade	red
	24th Brigade	yellow
1st Airborne Division	H.Q.	silver/black lines
	25th Brigade	white
	26th Brigade	red
	27th Brigade	yellow

10th Armoured Infantry Division (now Armoured Division)	H.Q.	silver/black lines
	28th Brigade	white
	29th Brigade	red
	30th Brigade	yellow
11th Armoured Infantry Division	H.Q.	silver/black lines
	31st Brigade	white
	32nd Brigade	red
	33rd Brigade	yellow
12th Armoured Division	H.Q.	silver/black lines
	34th Brigade	white
	35th Brigade	red
	36th Brigade	yellow

The average armoured division is formed by one armoured infantry (*Panzergrenadiere*) brigade and two armoured (*Panzer*) brigades, while the armoured infantry division is formed by two armoured infantry brigades and one armoured brigade. The rifle division has two rifle (*Jäger*) brigades and an armoured one, although the 2nd Rifle Division is still in the process of reorganisation.

The airborne division consists of three airborne (*Luftlande*) brigades and the mountain division is formed by two mountain (*Gebirgsjäger*) brigades and one armoured infantry brigade, which used to be an armoured mountain (*Geb. Pz.*) brigade.

All the formation badges, except that of the 1st Mountain Division, are shield-shaped and can be obtained in two versions: hand- and machine-embroidered.

German Democratic Republic

In January 1956, the People's Chamber of the G.D.R. sanctioned the establishment of the Ministry of National Defence and of the National People's Army (*Nationale Volksarmee* – N.V.A.) and in January 1962 legislation was passed which introduced general conscription. The Border Police came under the control of the Defence Ministry in September 1961.

The G.D.R. has been a member of the Warsaw Treaty since its establishment in May 1955; thus the N.V.A. automatically became associated with the armed forces of the U.S.S.R. and of the other Eastern European countries, under the united command of the member states of the Treaty.

The uniforms adopted by the N.V.A. are very similar in style to the traditional German uniforms which were in use until 1945, although the colour of the material is now different – stone-grey, the uniform collar being made of a darker material.

All ranks are entitled to wear service, walking-out, parade and field uniforms. They also have a double-breasted greatcoat with two rows of five buttons and a darker collar, buttoned up to the neck.

The ordinary tunic is single-breasted with five buttons and four patch pockets. The tunics of the walking-out and parade uniform have cuff patches and coloured piping on the cuffs. The officers have piping around the collar also. The tunic of the service uniform has no cuff patches and has piping only around the shoulder straps, which are the same for all uniforms.

All ranks can also wear an off-duty double-breasted jacket with open collar and two side pockets. Cuff patches are worn on this jacket, together with coloured piping around the cuffs and the top of the collar. This jacket is optional and must be bought privately if wanted.

The colour of the piping was the arm-of-service colour until 1962 but since then the uniform piping has been light green for the Border Troops and white for the rest of the army. The arm-of-service colours have been retained around the shoulder straps and on the collar and cuff patches only.

The peaked cap is worn with the service and walking-out uniforms: the side cap is usually worn by soldiers with service uniform and by all ranks with the field uniform. The helmet is worn by all ranks with the parade and field uniforms. The parachutists initially wore stone-grey berets; the beret worn with the parade and walking-out uniforms had white piping all around the sides. In 1968 they were issued with red berets. During the winter months all ranks wear a fur cap with folding sides together with the greatcoat.

The traditional mountain cap, with folding sides, was reintroduced in 1956 but a different mountain cap was adopted later. It is round, with folding sides joined at the top, and it also has a narrow cloth chin strap.

The standard Eastern European field uniform, made of striped cloth, is currently worn together with special camouflage overalls or utility garments.

In 1966 the sports overalls were adopted: the N.C.O.s wear a small silver-grey stripe on the left upper sleeve and the officers, two stripes.

Plate 67. Cap Badges

The national cockade surrounded by a wreath of oak leaves is worn on the peaked cap by all ranks; it is embroidered in gold wire for the generals and silver for officers, and made of white metal for the other ranks.

Initially the cockade consisted of the black, red and yellow national colours, later changed to the coat of arms of the G.D.R.

The generals wear gold twisted cords above the visor while the officers wear silver cords and the O.R.s wear a plain leather chin strap. The cap band is made of dark grey material with the exception of that of the Border Troops who wear light green cap bands, generals included. All other army generals wear red cap bands, and thus their cap badges are embroidered on red felt. A narrow coloured piping is worn around the crown of the peaked cap and on the upper side of the cap band.

The same type of cap badge is also used by all ranks on the mountain cap and by officers on the fur cap, while the O.R.s wear only the cockade on the latter. The cockade on its own is also worn on the side cap.

Breast Badges

A number of breast badges are worn by army personnel, usually above the right breast pocket of the tunic as the ribbons are worn on the other side.

All officers who have attended courses at the General Staff Academy and the Military Academy of the Soviet Army are entitled to wear special diamond-shaped badges made of metal and red and white enamel. They are both worn above any other badges already worn above the right breast pocket. The triangular badges of the Military Academy are also made of metal and enamel. As it is customary in the G.D.R. to name military institutions and units after socialist heroes, the Military Academy is named after Frederick Engels and his portrait is present in the centre of the badge. Similarly the portrait of Ernst-Moritz Arndt is on the badge of the Military Medical Section of the E.-M. Arndt University in Greifswald. The third badge is worn by officers who have graduated at a civilian university or high school.

Other badges are granted to individuals in order to stimulate their enthusiasm and keenness. The parachutist's badge is worn on the left breast.

Plate 68. Officers' Rank Badges

The N.V.A. officers display their rank on the shoulder straps, which in appearance conform with German military tradition.

The general's shoulder strap is made up of three interlaced cords, two gold and one silver, on which the individual rank is shown by five-pointed stars, or pips, made of silvered metal. Initially, in 1956, the stars were worn pointing outwards, whilst now they point inwards towards the collar. The backing material is red for army generals and light green for the generals of the Border Troops.

The senior officers' shoulder straps have two interlaced silver double cords while the junior officers wear the same silver cords straight, on a cloth underlay of arm-of-service colour. Both senior and junior officers' rank is shown by gold four-pointed stars.

The N.V.A. has three lieutenants' ranks in order to comply with Eastern European custom.

Medical officers now wear the Staff of Aesculapius on the shoulder straps, above the stars.

The officers and sergeants used to wear different rank insignia on the field uniform: these were stripes worn on the upper sleeves. At that time there were only three sergeants' ranks and, therefore, the Unteroffizier had one stripe, the Feldwebel two stripes and the Oberfeldwebel three stripes. The junior officers wore a thicker stripe with from one to four stripes above it, and the senior officers wore two thicker stripes with from one to three normal stripes above it. At present the usual rank badges are worn on the shoulder straps, but are embroidered in grey thread.

Plate 69. N.C.O.s' Rank Badges

In 1956 only three sergeants' ranks were adopted and only later, in 1962, were the ranks of Stabsfeldwebel and Unterfeldwebel added. From July 1960 until 1 January 1971 the Artillery sergeants had the title of Wachtmeister instead of Feldwebel: thus their rank titles were Stabswachtmeister, Oberwachtmeister, Wachtmeister and Unterwachtmeister. The infantry private was known as Schütze and the artillery private as Kanonier but, since 1971, all privates have been called Soldat.

An Oberfeldwebel can be appointed to the rank of Hauptfeldwebel (or Hauptwachtmeister) and consequently he can wear a stripe of lace above the cuffs. Corporals show their rank on the shoulder straps in the form of one or two silver stripes. The shoulder straps are typically Germanic, with rounded ends and piping in arm-of-service colours. Bandsmen wear the lyre on both straps, together with the usual rank badges.

Cadets' Rank Badges
The officer cadets have a silver stripe all around the loose sides of their shoulder straps on which they also wear a gothic 'S' made of white metal. The stripes at the outer ends of the shoulder straps represent the years of training and N.C.O. rank to which they are appointed (i.e. one stripe Unteroffizier, two stripes Feldwebel, etc.). The training to become an officer usually takes four years, the exception being medical officer training, which takes six years.

The N.C.O. cadet can be recognised by the coloured stripes he wears at the outer ends of the shoulder straps. The colour of the stripes matches the piping and shows the rank to which the cadet is appointed.

On 1 September 1956 a cadet school was opened for the training of young people and it existed until June 1960, when it was finally abolished. The boys wore army uniforms without collar patches and with a white metal 'K' on both shoulder straps. The junior cadets could reach the rank of Gefreiter and then wear a stripe of silver lace on the shoulder straps. The senior cadets wore a silver stripe at the front of the collar and around the shoulder straps, the Unteroffizier cadet wore the stripe around the loose sides of the straps, the Feldwebel cadet all around the shoulder straps with one silver star.

Service Stripes
The first pattern of service stripe was adopted in 1956: V-shaped chevrons worn on the left forearm. The one-stripe chevron was worn by personnel with more than three years' service; after five years' service the two-stripe chevron was worn.

On 1 January 1965 two different chevrons were introduced and are now worn on the right forearm. The one-stripe chevron is worn by soldiers who volunteer for three years service and the two-stripes chevron is worn by professional N.C.O.s, usually sergeants, who serve for a twelve-year period.

Plate 70. Patches/Arm-of-Service Colours
The generals of the N.V.A. wear the traditional German general's collar and cuff patches embroidered in gold. The collar patches of the generals of the Border Troops are embroidered on light green material while those of generals of the rest of the army are embroidered on red.

The officers and other ranks wear the traditional double bars on the collar and also on the cuffs of the 'dress' uniforms. The double bars are embroidered, woven or stitched on a background material the colour of which matches the material of the collar or cuffs.

The officers' collar and cuff patches are embroidered in silver while the other ranks wear grey woven patches or silver lace bars stitched on dark stone-grey patches. Some examples of each type have been illustrated. Initially the parachutists wore the same collar patches as the rest of the army, with white arm-of-service colour, from 1962 until autumn 1964 when the colour was changed to orange. On 1 November 1969 the patches were changed to the pattern illustrated. The officers wear the same patch with silver twisted cord piping all around.

The following are the arm-of-service colours:

white	Infantry (now Motorised Rifles)
red	Artillery and Rocket Troops
pink	Armoured Troops
black	Engineers, Chemical Service and all Technical Services
yellow	Signals
dark green	Medical, Legal and all other Non-Combatant Services
orange	Parachutists
light grey	Air Defence (and Missiles)
light green	Border Troops
olive-green	Pioneers

Plate 71. Miscellaneous Insignia

Both the proficiency and qualification badges are worn above the right breast pocket of the tunic and are awarded in three classes.

The Marksman lanyard is made of twisted matt silver cords and it is worn from the right shoulder to the second button of the tunic. Infantry, artillery and armour marksmanship are represented by different badges which are applied on the knot at the top of the lanyard. It is awarded in three classes which are distinguished by one (2nd class) and two (1st class) acorns.

There are three types of belt buckles: a gilded metal one for generals, and a silver for other officers, worn on the lace belt of the parade uniform, and the rectangular white metal buckle for other ranks. Officers wear a leather belt with plain Sam Browne type belt buckle with the service uniform.

Plate 72. Arm Badges

The badges illustrated are those worn at present on the left forearm of the tunic. The badges adopted initially were embroidered in yellow and were those of the medical and radio-location services now still in existence. There was also an oval badge for Helmsman, a round badge with a gothic

'F' for Artificier and another round badge with crossed guns for the Ordnance personnel. The first two were similar to those previously in use until 1945. Subsequently, the Helmsman badge was abolished and the other two were modified.

From 17 December 1957 to the beginning of 1966 the badges (Signals, Motor-Driver Technician, Radio Technician, Radio-Location, Medical, Armour and Reconnaissance) were embroidered in arm-of-service colours. Since 1966 all these badges have been machine-embroidered in silver thread, although there are also in existence hand-embroidered badges with silver piping all around the edges, for officers of the medical and legal services. The badge is now worn on the shoulder straps instead of on the arm.

Before November 1969 the parachutists wore an oval arm badge, depicting the parachute above the wings, which was later transferred onto the collar patches.

All ranks of the Guards Regiment stationed in Berlin wear white piping and officers' belt buckles, and on special occasions they wear white belts with cross strap. They also have a distinctive cuff title, with the inscription 'NVA-WACHREGIMENT', which they wear on the left sleeve.

U.S.S.R.

The Red Army of Workers and Peasants was renamed the Soviet Army in 1946. The Red Army traced its origins to the Red Guards, which were revolutionary formations active in Russia long before the 1917 Revolution. The Red Army was born officially in February 1918 and, although Russia had disentangled herself from World War 1, conscription was reintroduced in April 1918 in order to quell the anti-bolshevik movements and internal disorder.

Initially, the new army was mainly formed by infantry and, in order to create a separate striking force, all the cavalry units were gathered to form a Cavalry Corps which later, during the war against Poland, expanded into two Cavalry Armies.

The Red Army went through a period of redevelopment and mechanisation during the 1930s but it was during the Finnish War and subsequent World War 2 that Russian industrial resources, combined with battle experience, built the great military power which we know now. In 1945 the Red Army consisted of more than 500 infantry divisions, plus cavalry and artillery divisions, tank and mechanised corps (equivalent to divisions), anti-aircraft divisions and a great number of tank brigades and independent tank regiments.

In 1946 the STAVKA (Headquarters of the Supreme Commander of the Armed Forces) was replaced by the Military Council, and many other administrative changes and reorganisations have taken place since. In 1952 the airborne forces, previously under the Air Force, became a separate arm.

At the end of World War 2 officers of the Red Army were provided with a parade/walking-out uniform, an ordinary uniform and the field uniform. A white peaked cap and jacket were worn during summer in hot climates and a fur hat and greatcoat in winter.

The other ranks were issued with ordinary and field uniforms. The former were also used for parades and ceremonial occasions.

In April 1955 a new parade uniform was adopted by the marshals and generals: it was similar to the 1943 pattern but made of dark bluish-green material and now was double-breasted with two rows of six buttons. The gold ornamentation on the peaked cap, the shoulder boards and all the other details relating to the rank of the wearer remained the same.

In the following years an entirely new style of khaki uniform came into use. It was very similar to a civilian double-breasted suit; the jacket had an open collar with pointed lapels and two rows of three buttons. It was adopted in 1949 initially by the generals and officers of the Air Force and Armoured Corps, and it later became standard issue.

In April 1954 this new jacket, made of dark bluish-green material, was adopted by all the marshals and generals as a parade/walking-out uniform and with a khaki version for ordinary wear. During the following months summer uniforms in the same style were adopted as well; made of light grey material for the Marshal of the Soviet Union and white for the other marshals and generals. Later, in 1955, grey or khaki uniforms were adopted for all officers of the ground forces, including the generals whose dark bluish-green dress was replaced by a grey one.

The parade and the walking-out uniforms are very similar. For example the parade uniform of the marshals and generals consisted of the peaked cap with gold ornamentation, jacket, breeches and cavalry boots and was worn with decorations, medals and gold waist belt. The same dress, but with trousers instead of breeches, with medal ribbons only and without the waist belt, was the walking-out uniform.

The ordinary uniform consisted of the khaki peaked cap, khaki double-breasted jacket and dark blue trousers or breeches.

Three years later the officers' jacket was modified to the pattern which is in use currently: it is single-breasted with four buttons and without pointed lapels. The cuff patches have been abolished and the badges considerably simplified.

By a decree of 26 July 1969 of the Ministry of Defence, the uniforms of the officers and long-serving N.C.O.s were divided into service/parade and parade/walking-out uniforms, plus the ordinary and field uniforms.

The other ranks (conscripted N.C.O.s and soldiers) have a parade/walking-out uniform, the ordinary uniform and the field uniform.

Although the shirt-tunic is still worn, it has been widely replaced by some more comfortable jackets and tunics. The O.R.s' khaki jacket is similar to that of the officers, with an open collar showing shirt and tie and without breast pockets. It is worn together with the helmet, breeches and high boots, with the personal weapons for parade duties and with the peaked cap and trousers as a walking-out uniform.

A tunic with buttoned-up folded collar, and without breast pockets, is worn together with forage cap as the other ranks' ordinary uniforms, which is the only uniform usually possessed by the conscripted other ranks.

The airborne troops wear light blue berets, light blue collar patches and shoulder straps.

New field uniforms have also been adopted for winter and summer and special overalls are worn by airborne and armoured troops. The fur hat and greatcoat are still worn during winter.

Plate 73. Service Chevrons (26 November 1945)

The first decree on dress regulations to be published after World War 2 appropriately granted service chevrons to be worn on the left upper sleeve, just above the elbow, by the war veterans. The chevrons consisted of silver or gold stripes of lace, 15 or 25 mm. in width, V-shaped at an angle of 95–105 degrees. One narrow silver chevron was worn after one year's service, one wide silver chevron was added after the second year, one narrow gold one after the third and a wide gold one after the fifth year of service.

Shoulder Boards

On 31 January 1947, due to the post-war reorganisation of the Soviet Army, the generals and officers of the Reserve and Retired Lists were distinguished from those in active service by the adoption of 28-mm. lace stripes worn across the shoulder boards. The reservists wore plain stripes while the others had a zigzag motif woven on the same stripe as the former: silver stripes were worn on gold shoulder boards and vice-versa.

Arm Badges

Two new arm badges were authorised, for parachutists and personnel of the Railway Military Transport, on 18 August 1947 and 13 February 1951 respectively.

The badge of the parachutists measures 5.5 × 11 cm. and the winged parachutist in its centre 3.7 × 8 cm., and the surrounding edging is 2.5 mm. wide. The badge is worn on the left upper sleeve.

The badge of the Railway Military Transport was 4.5 × 10.5 cm. in size, surrounded by a 2-mm. edging all around.

Plate 74. Railway Military Transport

The railway system has always been the most important, vital service of Russia due to the vastness of its territory. As early as 1919 the personnel of the railways wore their own special badge on a red armband which, together with the red star, is one of the first badges to have been officially adopted by the Red Army. The badge is the winged wheel, then made in white metal and affixed on a diamond-shaped patch with yellow or green edging. Later, during World War 2, the same badge, always on the diamond-shaped patch, was worn on the left upper sleeve of the uniform and the winged wheel, on its own, on the red crown of the peaked cap. Small metal winged wheels were also worn as collar badges before 1936.

A new badge, for wearing on the sleeve and on the collar, was adopted in 1936 by the combined Railway–Road–Waterways Communications Service. It depicted a star superimposed on an anchor and crossed hammer and spanner, with side wings.

On 13 February 1951 new regulations prescribed the wearing of the composite badge described above on the arm and shoulder straps and of the winged wheel on the crown of the peaked cap, above the red star. New collar patches and cap bands were adopted as well, in the colours previously used by the engineers in the 1920s: black with blue piping. The new arm badge therefore is mounted on a diamond-shaped backing (4.5 × 10.5 mm.) which is black with blue edging, and blue piping surrounds the shoulder boards.

Service Chevrons

New service chevrons were authorised on 31 March 1952 for personnel serving longer than their period of conscription. One narrow gold chevron was awarded for the first two years of re-enlistment, and two narrow chevrons for the next two years. One wide gold chevron was worn by personnel re-enlisting for a further period of from four to ten years' service and, finally, two wide chevrons were awarded to personnel who served for over ten years. The narrow lace stripe was 10 mm. in width, the wide one 25 mm., and the finished chevron was 10 cm. in length.

Parade and Ordinary Uniforms (9 April 1954)

The jackets of the pattern already introduced in 1949 were adopted by the marshals and generals in 1954 as part of the dark bluish-green parade/walking-out uniforms and khaki ordinary uniforms (as described in the introduction to this section). The Marshal of the Soviet Union had an oak leaf motif embroidered in gold on the collar and cuffs of the dark bluish-green jacket, while the other marshals and generals had a laurel leaf motif, combined in both cases with double gold piping and red piping.

The khaki ordinary uniform did not have gold-embroidered trimmings. Instead it was worn with collar patches and a red piping on the peaked cap, collar and cuffs of the jacket. The Marshal of the Soviet Union wore red patches with gilded buttons surrounded on three sides by gold piping, and the other marshals and generals patches in arm-of-service colour with gilded buttons and gold piping.

Plate 75. Lapels and Cuffs

On 10 June 1954 new regulations were issued and during that summer new ordinary uniforms were introduced for the top ranking officers. Those of the Marshal of the Soviet Union were made of light grey material and the others of khaki. Gold oak and laurel motifs replaced the patches on the collar and the small left breast pocket of the previous jacket was ultimately abolished.

The same style of uniform, similar to a civilian double-breasted suit, was officially adopted by all officers on 25 February 1955. It came in two versions: grey for parade/walking-out uniforms and khaki for ordinary wear.

A leaf ornamentation was present on the collar and on the cuffs of the former, with gilded collar badges, while collar patches with the arm-of-service badge at the apex were worn on the khaki uniform. The officers of the armoured troops had black facing around the collar of the grey uniform.

Visors, Chin Straps and Belts

The regulations of 10 June 1954, previously mentioned, also prescribed gold ornamentation on the visor of the peaked caps.

Gold and silver cords were authorised in 1940 for the Marshal of the Soviet Union and generals, together with new round cap badges. Three years later the oak and laurel motifs were adopted, embroidered on cap bands, collars and cuffs. On 20 February 1949 the officers of the armoured troops were granted one row of gold oak leaves on the visor of the parade peaked cap, the marshals and generals of the same service with the addition of a double gold piping around the rim.

Thus in the summer of 1954, the same ornamentation was granted to the marshals and generals of the rest of the army.

Gold waist belts with gilded belt buckles were adopted on 25 February 1955 as part of the marshals' and officers' parade uniform.

Plate 76. Parade Peaked Caps (1955)

The ornamentation of the peaked cap was modified further by some new regulations during 1955.

The new oval cap badge (see also Plate 83) was adopted on 25 February 1955 to be worn on its own on the cap band of the officers' khaki ordinary peaked cap. This peaked cap has a black leather visor and chin strap. A gold twin-cord chin strap was added to the officers' grey peaked cap of the parade/walking-out uniform and the cap badge was now applied onto an ornament of gold leaves. The gold ornamentation was adopted on the visor the previous year.

On 3 March 1955 a new gold chin strap was introduced for the grey peaked cap of the parade/walking-out uniform of marshals and generals. The new oval cap badge was applied on the gold oak or laurel leaves ornamentation already adopted in 1943. The same regulations also prescribed an ornamentation of gold oak leaves on the visor of the grey peaked cap of the Marshal of the Soviet Union and an ornamentation of laurel leaves on that of the other marshals and generals.

All marshals and generals have the new cap badge on a plain red cap band, together with gold cords and black leather visor, on the ordinary khaki peaked cap.

Plate 77. Arm-of-Service Badges (1955)

These small badges are worn on the shoulder straps or on the collar patches and show the branch of service of the wearer. They are considerably different from those used during the War, even for the branches of service which still exist today. A tank, for instance, is still the badge of the armoured troops, but it is an entirely different tank from that previously used.

Often one badge is worn by personnel of several different services, as in the case of the crossed hammer and spanner of the technical troops, worn by chemical and smoke units (toxic, smoke producing and incendiary warfare), electric line-of-communications layers and technical engineers. The badge of the Engineers–Technical Troops is worn by fitters, builders and maintenance units. All these badges were authorised on 23 June 1955.

Collar Patches for Overcoat (23 June 1955)

A new overcoat was introduced for summer wear in June 1955 and some special collar patches (7.5 cm. in length) were authorised at the same time. The marshals and generals were granted gold or silver piping on three sides of the patch. That of the Marshal of the Soviet Union had a golf leaf motif; the others had a laurel leaf motif. The marshals and generals of the non-combatant services (Medical, Veterinary and Legal) had a silver motif and silver piping.

On 1 August 1955 similar collar patches were adopted for the officers' overcoat, worn with arm-of-service badges at their apex. Such patches were made only in three colours, raspberry-red, black and dark green, which do not necessarily match the colours of the marshals' and generals' services. The branch of service of the wearer was further distinguished by its badge.

Plate 78. Orchestra of the Regimental Garrison at Moscow (11 March 1955)

The musicians of this orchestra had a special parade uniform with red cap bands, shoulder boards and cuffs, and blue piping. Their tunics were double-breasted with six buttons on two rows, and white waist belts.

They also wore the Bandsman badge, the lyre, on the peaked cap and on the collar.

The Honorary Guards (1 August 1955)

All ranks of this unit were issued with new parade uniforms in August 1955. These uniforms were grey, with red cap bands on the peaked cap and with red collar, shoulder boards and cuffs and red plastron edged by a stripe of gold lace, on the double-breasted tunic. Similar trimmings used to be part of the Russian Guards' uniforms before World War 1.

Later, the Soviet Guards adopted khaki uniforms slightly modified. The other ranks had only the red star on the cap band and the tunic lost the red cuffs and collar. The latter is now khaki with red patches. The plastron remained the same, but the gold piping and the regimental number is no longer worn on the red shoulder boards.

Plates 79 and 80. Officers' Rank Badges
Parade and Walking-Out Uniforms

Since the introduction of the jacket with open collar, the inner ends of the shoulder boards were covered by the collar. Thus the shape of the inner part of them became irrelevant and the button was discarded.

New regulations issued on 22 September 1956 prescribed a new shape of shoulder boards for the marshals and on 29 March 1958 the same were extended to the generals and officers as well.

In 1958 new khaki parade/walking-out and ordinary uniforms were adopted for the officers and sergeants. The new jackets were single-breasted with four buttons and an open collar showing the shirt and tie, and without breast pockets. Coloured piping was abolished and all the badges considerably simplified.

The shoulder boards illustrated in this plate and the first four in the following plate all belong to the parade and walking-out uniforms and are woven in gold or silver.

The coat of arms on the shoulder boards of the Marshal of the Soviet Union are 47 mm. in width and the star, embroidered in gold on red background, is 50 mm. in diameter.

The rank badge of the Supreme Marshals is a gold star 40 mm. in diameter surrounded by a wreath, while the marshals wear only the star. Both wear the arm-of-service badge also, on the shoulder boards, and piping and edging around the star in the colour of their branch of service.

The marshals' and generals' shoulder boards are 65 mm. in width, the officers', only 60 mm. The generals and officers of non-combatant services have silver boards with rank stars and badges made of gold, the others have gold shoulder boards and silver stars and badges.

Plate 80. Officers' Rank Badges
Ordinary Uniforms

On 29 March 1958 new shoulder boards were also introduced for all ranks' ordinary uniforms: plain officers' shoulder boards had already been introduced in December 1956 for use on the ordinary, sports and field uniforms. The background of the new shoulder straps matches the colour of the ordinary uniform; the stars and other badges are gold.

Also conventional shoulder boards with buttons have been made for wearing on tunics and shirt-tunics.

The arm-of-service badges are worn on the shoulder boards or on the collar patches, depending on the type of uniform or by the rank of the wearer. They are never worn on both the shoulder boards and collar of the same uniform.

Plate 81. Officers' Rank Badges
Field Uniform

The shoulder boards for field uniforms were also adopted on 29 March 1958 and are always worn on tunics. They are very similar to those of the ordinary uniform but with the rank stars and badges made of tarnished metal. The coat of arms of the Marshal of the Soviet Union is the only fully coloured badge worn on the shoulder boards of this uniform.

N.C.O.s' Rank Badges
Parade/Walking-Out and Ordinary/Field Uniforms

The coloured shoulder boards for the parade/walking-out uniforms were adopted on 30 December 1955 and were similar to those previously worn except for the piping, which was abolished. The arm-of-service badges used to be worn pinned below the rank stripes, whilst after the new regulations they had to be worn above the stripes, below the button.

Coloured boards with gold stripes and badges were worn on parade/ walking-out uniforms, khaki boards with red stripes and tarnished badges on the others.

The 29 March 1958 regulations granted the use of an officers' jacket to the regular sergeants (serving longer than the period of conscription) also, and new shoulder boards were adopted as well. The gold rank stripes were replaced by khaki stripes and the arm-of-service badges were transferred onto the collar, pinned on collar patches. The tarnished metal badges were still worn on the shoulder boards of the field uniform.

The rank insignia of the Sergeant-Major was modified in 1963 (Plate 82).

Plate 82. Cap Badges and Lapels

On 29 March 1958 new khaki uniforms were adopted for officers and sergeants as parade/walking-out and ordinary uniforms. The jackets were single-breasted with four buttons, with an open collar showing the shirt and tie, and without breast pockets. Coloured piping was abolished and all the badges were considerably simplified.

The officers retained their oval cap badges, with the red star in its centre: it is worn on the peaked cap of the parade/walking-out uniform together with a metal wreath which replaces all the gold ornamentation adopted in 1955, with the exception of the gold cord chin strap. The oval badge, which is made of red and white enamel and anodised gold, is worn on its own on the coloured cap band of the ordinary peaked cap, with a black leather chin strap. The same cap badge but in a colour matching the peaked cap was adopted for the field uniform peaked cap, which has a khaki visor and chin strap.

The cap badge of the other ranks is the red star which is worn together with a gold anodised metal wreath, as is that of the officers, on the peaked cap of the parade/walking-out uniforms.

New oak and laurel motifs of the marshals' and generals' ordinary uniforms were adopted, made of tarnished metal instead of the gold ones adopted in 1954. The officers and sergeants (later all ranks) adopted raspberry-red or black patches, with arm-of-service badges, on the collar of the khaki jackets. A narrow gold piping was added on three sides of the patch worn on parade/walking-out uniform, plain patches on the ordinary uniform.

Shoulder Boards and Service Chevrons

Until 1963 the Sergeant-Major wore a large and a thinner stripe arranged in a T shape but since that year his rank has been identified by only a large stripe, worn all along the centre of his shoulder boards.

The Russian soldier now wears the brass letters 'C A', which stand for the initials of the Soviet Army, at the outer ends of the shoulder boards of his greatcoat and of all uniforms except field.

A Warrant Officer rank was created on 1 January 1972 with two stars on the shoulder boards, and provision is made for the future establishment of a Junior W.O. rank with only one star. The Warrant Officer wears also service chevrons on the left lower sleeve, above the cuff. They are made of gold lace stripes on red background. One narrow chevron is added for each year of service until three are reached. The fourth year is represented by a large chevron and a gold star is added for service between five and nine years. On the tenth year and over a large chevron below two stars is worn. These chevrons are not worn on the field uniform.

Breast Badges

The Extended Service badge was adopted on 1 August 1957. It is made of metal and enamel, 26 × 60 mm. in size, and a small triangular plaque attached below the badge shows the number of years of service it is awarded for.

Later, another wing-shaped badge was introduced for the tank crews, divided into four classes, the top class with an 'M' in the centre of the shield.

The badge of Infantry Specialist, the Proficiency badge and all other badges of this type are usually worn on the right breast of the jacket or tunic.

Plate 83. Arm Badges (1972)

The shield-shaped arm badges were introduced in 1972 and are worn on the left upper sleeve of the jacket and greatcoat. They are all similar in design, with the branch-of-service badge in the centre, all on a background of arm-of-service colour. The branch-of-service badges in most cases are similar to those previously used on the collar and shoulder boards, although new badges were introduced in order to distinguish the various specialities of the technical troops.

The Traffic Controller wears a round badge with a yellow 'P' enclosed in a shield-shaped border.

Belgium

The present Belgian Army is descended from the army of 1940, whose traditions were loyally maintained through the war years by the Belgian forces raised in the United Kingdom. They were considerably reinforced during the closing months of the War after the liberation of Belgium. At the same time, between January and June 1945, another five infantry brigades, each comprising 4,300 men, were raised and sent to Northern Ireland for training.

An agreement was signed on 1 December 1944 between SHAEF and the Belgian Government, by which Belgium provided the Liberated Manpower Units (L.M.U.) that, equipped by Britain, were used to maintain the Allied line of communications. However, several of these units also fought bravely beside British, American and Canadian troops.

When peace came at last, the Belgian troops were wearing British uniforms with the traditional Belgian badges.

The khaki battledress was the field uniform of all ranks. The officers, warrant officers and sergeants also had another uniform which consisted of a jacket with four patch pockets, shoulder straps and open collar showing the shirt and tie, peaked cap and trousers. This uniform, with slight variations, was worn for various duties and special occasions. It was worn as full dress uniform, together with white shirt and black tie, decorations and medals, shoulder cords instead of shoulder straps and, in the case of officers, with lace waist belt also. For ceremonial duties it was worn with white shirt and black tie and lace waist belt and ribbons instead of metal decorations. A khaki shirt and tie and the Sam Browne belt, or a plain khaki cloth belt, were worn with the walking-out uniform.

Officers and warrant officers wore battledress with peaked caps as their service dress; with the beret or steel helmet as field uniform. They both had the battledress blouse with open collar, while the O.R.s' blouse was buttoned up to the neck.

The webbing equipment was khaki, the exception being the webbing of military policemen, regimental policemen and bandsmen who had white webbing. The Chasseurs of the Ardennes wore their traditional green berets, tankmen wore black berets, parachutists maroon berets and the rest of the army, khaki berets.

Plate 84. Generals' and Senior Officers' Rank Badges

Belgian rank badges did not change a great deal after World War 2 and are still worn on the collar patches, with the exception of the generals who also wear stars on the shoulder straps. Different chin-strap cords, bars and bands on the peaked cap distinguish the classes of rank.

All ranks wear the Belgian national cockade on the peaked cap. There are now three ranks of generals, all wearing amaranth red cap bands with two gold double bars and gold piping around their base, and gold chin strap on the peaked cap. They also have the 'thunderbolt' badge, unique to their rank, on the cap and on the collar patches; on the latter it is worn together with gold-embroidered double bars and stars. Their collar patches are black with a 2-mm. amaranth piping at the top.

All the senior officers, including the Colonel-Brigadier, wear two single vertical bars, gold or silver chin-strap cords and piping on the peaked cap and, in the case of the Colonel-Brigadier, an additional coloured cap band. At the front, between the bars, the arm-of-service badge is worn pinned or embroidered above the chin strap.

As the different corps have different patches and different badges, the collar patches illustrated only depict the rank of a particular corps. The rank of Colonel is represented by a patch of a Colonel of Infantry who has qualified at the Staff College: thus he wears the infantry patch with the G.S. badge, known as *demi-foudre*. Next are the collar patches of a Lieutenant-Colonel of the Engineers and of a Major of the Grenadiers. The Grenadiers wear a gold flaming grenade on the scarlet blue-piped collar patches of the infantry.

All ranks of the Infantry and Artillery respectively wear scarlet patches with royal blue piping and royal blue patches with scarlet piping, without the arm-of-service badges, which however are worn on the peaked cap and on the shoulder straps. Thus I have illustrated the crown of the Infantry and the crossed cannons of the Artillery as worn on the peaked cap by a Colonel-Brigadier and by a senior officer of these corps.

Plate 85. Junior Officers' and Warrant Officers' Rank Badges

All ranks of the Cavalry and the warrant officers and sergeants of all corps wear silver or white metal insignia (badges, chin-strap cords, stars, etc.) while the rest of the army wears gilded or brass insignia.

Both junior officers and warrant officers wear gold or silver chin-strap cords on the peaked cap. Officers wear six-pointed stars on the collar patches and the 1st Captain, in some corps known as Captain Commandant, has the three stars of the captains surrounded by a thin (2 × 30 mm.) horizontal bar. Warrant officers wear silver badges: the W.O. one silver star and the W.O. 1st Class, the star below a small bar (2 × 16 mm.).

Other Collar Patches

The personnel of the Legal Service wear royal blue patches with ultra-marine blue piping on which they wear the appointment badge above a gold bar 30 mm. in length. The Judge Advocate General and the Judge Advocate wear the *faisceau de licteur* surrounded by wreaths of oak and laurel respectively, above a thick bar, whilst the Clerks of the Legal Service wear only the *faisceau de licteur* without wreath, above a thin bar.

The Ingenieurs des Fabrications Militaire are officers specialised in mechanics, electronics, etc., who study and control the production of equipment supplied to the army. They have royal blue collar patches with scarlet piping, the usual stars and bars and the cogwheel on crossed hammers badge.

Finally, a collar patch for other ranks of the Medical Service, in the shape as worn by the other ranks of all corps on the collar of the battle-dress blouse, is illustrated.

The colours of the remaining patches are as follows:

	Patch	Piping
Infantry of the Line, Grenadiers	scarlet red	royal blue
Carabiniers, Chasseurs-on-Foot	dark green	yellow
Chasseurs of the Ardennes	dark green	scarlet
Security Sections	dark green	black
Commandos	black	white
Parachutists	maroon	sky-blue
Guides	amaranth-red	green
Lancers	white	royal blue
Chasseurs-on-Horse	yellow	royal blue
Artillery, Royal Military School, Cadets School	royal blue	scarlet
Engineers	black	scarlet
Signals	black	green
R.A.S.C.	ultramarine	orange
R.E.M.E.	black	orange
Military Police	scarlet	white
Doctors	amaranth	amaranth
Pharmacists	emerald-green	green
Stomatologists	dark violet	amaranth
Veterinaries	ultramarine	royal blue
Medical Service (O.R.s)	amaranth	royal blue
R.A.O.C.	grey	amaranth
Commissariat	royal blue	sky-blue
Administrative Service	royal blue	grey-blue

The officers and warrant officers of the Engineers and Signals, and the Doctors, Pharmacists, Stomatologists and Veterinaries (all officers) have velvet collar patches, while the patches of all the others, including generals, are made of felt.

Badges are worn on the collar patches in order to specify a particular appointment, rank or service (G.S. Officers, Advocates and Clerks of the Legal Services, Commissaries, etc.) or in order to distinguish one corps from another in the case when both wear the same patch. The Grenadiers, for instance, wear an infantry patch with the grenade, and the Carabiniers wear the same patch as the Chasseurs-on-Foot, but with an additional bugle.

The Engineers wear the traditional helmet as their badge.

Most of the arm-of-service badges illustrated in the following plates are worn on the shoulder straps and on the collar of the greatcoat.

Plate 86. Sergeants' and Corporals' Rank Badges

The sergeants and corporals of the Belgian Army wear rank stripes on both forearms, above the cuffs, pointing inwards at a 30-degree angle. Khaki stripes are worn on the field uniform and silver ones, considerably smaller, are worn on the other uniforms. Regular sergeants and bandsmen, and all ranks of the Military Police, wear the peaked cap with a brown leather chin strap, while corporals and privates are entitled to wear the peaked cap, with khaki cloth chin strap, only after ten and fifteen years of active service respectively. No rank badges are worn on the beret.

Front Line Wound Stripes and Service Chevrons

The stripes are worn in the same manner as the rank stripes but on the left upper sleeve: they are made of gold or silver lace and each measures 4 × 40 mm. The chevron is also 4 mm. in width and each arm is 32 mm. in length, with a 120-degree angle between the arms, and it is worn on the left sleeve.

Armlets

There are two police organisations in the Belgian Army: the Military Police, which is an independent organisation, and the Regimental Police, whose personnel is part of the various regiments and units.

The military policemen have their own badges, white webbing equipment, armlets and peaked caps with a red cover, when on duty. The regimental policemen wear only white webbing equipment and the armlet when on duty, together with the badges of the corps and regiment they belong to.

The armlets of both organisations are black with red letters 'PM' and

'PR', standing for Police Militaire and Police Régimentaire respectively. Both measure 6 × 39 cm.

Plate 87. Miscellaneous Badges
Royal Military School's Shoulder Cords and Badges

The cadets of the Royal Military School wear plaited cord colours at the shoulder indicating the year of the course. All cadets wear a sprig of laurel in white metal (2.8 × 1 cm.) and the qualified N.C.O. instructors wear two sprigs of laurel instead. The Polytechnic Branch of the same school wear a diamond-shaped badge, 3 × 3 cm. in size.

The students of other training schools wear coloured bands, slipped on the outer ends of the shoulder straps. The Physical Training Instructors have two badges: the N.C.O. instructors wear a sword (5 × 1.6 cm.), while the officers wear two crossed swords and the crown.

Three types of Belgian wings, the badge of the Commandos Training Centre, and the wing worn by parachute instructors, have also been illustrated.

Plate 88. Formation Signs

Most formation signs depict the Belgian Lion, or just his face, the exception being those of the parachutists and commandos which were adopted in Britain during the War. Formation signs are worn on the left upper sleeve of the battledress.

The badge of the Ground Forces Base was adopted in February 1959 and depicts the Lion's head on a shield divided into the colours of the five components of that organisation: Engineers, Signals, Quartermasters, Ordnance and Security Section. In 1969 it was replaced by another sign showing a hand supporting a sword which suggests the role of this logistical organisation.

The round formation sign is no longer worn as the Home Defence Forces now wear the sign of the former 2nd Corps.

The Lion's head appears on all the divisional signs, on a different coloured background for each division. The amaranth and white of the 16th Armoured Division's badge are the colours of the Guides and Lancers whose regiments originally composed the division.

Arm-of-Service Badges

The badges illustrated in this and the two following plates could be divided into corps and service badges, and appointment badges, known in Belgium as *Attributs des Fonctions*. They are worn at the front of the peaked cap, some on the shoulder straps, some on the collar patches and also on the collar of the greatcoat.

The badges illustrated in this plate are worn by officers only. That of the generals is known as *foudre* (thunderbolt), and that of the General Staff as *demi-foudre*. The latter is worn on the collar patches of the corps of service of the wearer.

The Commissaries and the Doctors, Veterinaries and Pharmacists wear their gold badges on the cap and collar and their unit's badge on the shoulder straps. The cadets of the three latter services wear a silver badge and the 2nd Lieutenant cadet wears the officer's gold badge but with a silver mirror.

The badge of the Substitute Judge Advocates has a silver axe.

Plate 89. Arm-of-Service Badges

Silver and white metal badges are worn by the cavalry and by the warrant officers and sergeants of all corps, gilded and brass badges by personnel of the rest of the army.

Many new badges have been introduced since the War and the structure of the army has also been modified and modernised. However, most of the old badges are still used nowadays, such as the crown of the Infantry of the Line, the bugle of the Carabiniers and Chasseurs-on-Foot, and the beautiful badge, the boar's head, of the Chasseurs of the Ardennes. Among the cavalry badges only that of the Chasseurs-on-Horse has been modified, as previously it depicted a sword across a bugle. The badges of the Artillery and Engineers remain those in use before World War 2.

Some badges were introduced during or soon after the War when the Belgian Army was connected with the British Army and new corps were formed as a result.

The Pioneers badge is now a skill-at-arms badge and is worn on the sleeve.

Plate 90. Arm-of-Service Badges

There are three types of badges worn by different categories of Clerks of the Legal Service. One is made of gold, one is gold with a silver axe, and a third is all made of silver. The warrant officers and sergeants of the Medical, Veterinary and Pharmacist Service wear silver badges, the lower ranks brass badges.

The Logistical Corps (CORLOG) has been formed recently by the amalgamation of the Quartermasters and Ordnance Corps. The helmet on crossed cannons badge was worn in the early 1950s by personnel of the Tank battalions attached to the infantry divisions; the badge is now obsolete.

Shoulder-Strap Numerals

Some examples of units using Arabic and Roman numerals have been illustrated. They are all 19 mm. in height and are made of brass or white metal; divisional numerals are on a rectangular background (26 × 22 mm.) and brigade numerals are on a disc (27 mm. in diameter).

Beret Badges

The beret is worn as a complement to the battledress and in general it is the head-dress usually worn by the soldiers. The Chausseurs of the Ardennes wear dark green berets, parachutists, maroon berets, personnel of the armoured units, black, and personnel of the Army Aviation, light blue. Khaki berets are worn by the personnel of the rest of the army.

The badges are made of different metals depending on the rank or corps of the wearer and most are worn on a shield-shaped coloured backing, with the exception of those worn on coloured berets.

The badges of the Infantry of the Line, Grenadiers, Artillery and Military Police, for instance, are worn on a red backing, the badges of the Royal Military School, Cadets School, R.A.S.C., Signals and Administrative Service on a blue backing, dark blue for the badge of the latter. The beret badges of the Engineers and R.E.M.E. have a black backing and that of the R.A.O.C. a grey backing; the Medical badge is worn on an amaranth backing and the Carabiniers wear a green backing. The Chasseurs-on-Horse have yellow, the Lancers white and the Guides amaranth backings.

Beret Badges

The beret badges of the R.A.S.C., of the R.E.M.E. and of the R.A.O.C. are not in use anymore. The former, with the motto 'VICTORIAM ALO', was worn for a time by the Quartermasters which later joined the personnel of the R.A.O.C. to form the new Logistical Corps. The Engineers and signallers used to wear similar badges but now a new badge has been adopted by the Signals.

Plate 91. Beret Badges
Chasseurs-on-Horse

Five regiments of Chasseurs-on-Horse have existed since the War; the badge of the 5th Regiment is that of the 2nd with the figure '5' below the scroll. The 1st and 2nd Chasseurs-on-Horse were formed in 1830 from former hussars regiments. The 2nd Regiment, for instance, was raised by Prince Victor Philip de Croy on 1 March 1814 and after the disband-ment of the Belgian Legion of Napoleon's army, it became the 8th Hussars Regiment of the Army of the Netherlands, and subsequently the 2nd Chasseurs on Horse of the new Belgian Army.

The 3rd Regiment originates from the 3rd Lancers and existed briefly in the 1920s: it was re-raised in 1952 together with the 4th which, formed in 1913, was in existence during World War 1. The 5th was formed in 1957.

Guides

The 1st and 2nd Regiments of Guides were raised in 1830 and 1874 respectively. The former was originally known as the Cossacks of the Meuse, and became a regiment of guides on 24 January 1833. The 1st Regiment was reformed on 8 March 1946 from the Armoured Car Regiment and retains the traditions of the former Armoured Squadron of the Belgian Forces in the U.K.

The 2nd Regiment was re-formed in 1952, the 3rd was raised in 1957 and the 4th in 1961.

Lancers

The 1st and 2nd Lancers were formed in 1830 by the Provisional Belgian Government, although the former traces its origins to the Van Der Burch Light Cavalry, raised in 1814. The 3rd was raised in 1830 as a regiment of cuirassiers, converted to lancers on 1 January 1863. The 2nd Lancers was reformed in 1949 and the 3rd the year after.

The 4th Lancers was, until 1863, the 2nd Regiment of Cuirassiers which was raised in 1836.

The modern 4th, 5th, 6th, 7th and 8th Lancers were all formed in 1952; the 9th and 10th in 1961, but the former wore the beret badge of the 4th Heavy Tanks Battalion.

The 5th Lancers was raised in 1913, disbanded in 1923 and reformed in 1939. The 6th Lancers descended from the 2nd Lancers, became a regiment on 1 January 1920 and disbanded three years later.

Plate 92. Beret Badges
Infantry

Thirteen infantry regiments have been raised since the end of the War. However a beret badge for the 10th Infantry Regiment does not exist, as before the war this unit became the Regiment of Chasseurs of the Ardennes and adopted the boar's head as its insignia. The 13th existed for only a few months after the War. The 6th Infantry Regiment has worn in turn two badges, both of which are illustrated.

The grenades of the Grenadiers and the Mortar Company are worn on a red backing as these units are part of the infantry.

Three regiments of Chasseurs-on-Foot, each wearing different badges, have existed since the War and each of the three para-commando battalions wears a different badge. The 3rd Parachute Battalion is famous for its participation in the Korean War. The Chasseurs of the Ardennes exist at present as battalions, not as a regiment. The 'B' in the centre of the Carabiniers badge stands for the King's name, Baudouin.

Plate 93. Beret Badges
Schools and Training/Armoured Units

These badges are worn on patches of their own arm-of-service colour, blue in the case of the Royal Military School and Cadets School. The badge of the Armoured Troops Training Centre can be worn on yellow, white or crimson backing by chasseurs, lancers and guides respectively.

The Armoured School traces its origins to a cavalry school created in 1842 at Brussels and, after many changes and conversions, it became the School for Armoured Troops in 1945.

The Armoured Troops Training Centre and the Armoured Troops Demonstration Detachment were formed in 1951 and amalgamated in 1961. The latter was an international establishment, thus the letters 'JTTC' in the scroll stand for Joint Tank Training Center, which was a Belgian–American establishment. A similar badge, but without the scroll, was worn by the personnel of the Armoured Centre (1954–8).

The 1st Heavy Tanks Battalion was created in 1951 as the armoured support of the 1st Infantry Division. The first badge illustrated on the left was never worn and the second was later replaced by a third pattern.

The personnel of this battalion wore the knight's helmet on crossed cannons on the peaked cap and on the shoulder straps. The 4th Heavy Tanks Battalion was created on 1 April 1952 as part of the 4th Infantry Division and was subsequently disbanded in 1956.

The 1st and 4th Reconnaissance Squadrons of the 1st and 4th Infantry Divisions were also formed in the early 1950s, each with its own beret badge, with squadron number, on white backing. In 1953 both adopted a badge without a squadron number.

Bibliographical Note

Among the many publications which could further enlarge one's knowledge of the subject I have dealt with, I would like to mention the following:

> *Regimental Badges*, by Major T. Edwards, several volumes (later revised and edited by A. L. Kipling), dealing with British cap badges.
> *Heraldry in War* and *Badges on Battledress*, both by Lt-Col. H. N. Cole, in several revised editions, dealing with British formation signs.
> *Military Badge Collecting* by J. Gaylor, dealing with British cap badges.
> *German Army Uniforms and Insignia*, by B. L. Davis.
> *Orders, Decorations, Medals and Badges of the 3rd Reich*, by Littlejohn and Dodkins.
> *Uniforms of the SS*, a series by A. Mollo and other authors, illustrating in great detail the uniforms, badges and equipment of the German SS.
> *American Badges and Insignia*, by E. E. Kerrigan.
> *Emblemes de Cavalerie*, by J. P. Champagne, a very good publication on Belgian cavalry badges (Editions G. Everling, Arlon).
> *Żołnierz Polski*, by K. Linder, H. Wiewióra and T. Woźnicki, an illustrated book, showing Polish uniforms and badges used in the period 1939–65 (Wydawnictwo Ministerstwa Obrony Narodowej, Warsaw).
> *Uniformi Militari Italiane*, by E. and V. Giudice, Volumes I and II, dealing with all the Italian uniforms worn from 1861 to 1968 (Bramante Editrice, Milan).

Other good publications on military subjects might be available and I do not list them solely because I do not know them, or because they do not concern the armies I have dealt with in my own books.

As a member of the American Society of Military Insignia Collectors I have gained much useful information from their remarkable periodical, *Trading Post*. I would also like to mention the marvellous pamphlets of the Military Heraldry Society.

Index

*This is not a complete index but is intended only as a
cross reference between illustrations and description*